AF846566

CLODAGH AT HOME

OVER 120 RECIPES & STORIES FROM THE FARM FOR EFFORTLESS ENTERTAINING

CLODAGH McKENNA

KYLE BOOKS

CONTENTS

WELCOME TO MY HOME

Broadspear, for me, has always been a forever home. Not a showpiece or a project with an end date, but a place that holds all the seasons of a life: muddy boots and big parties, quiet mornings and fun nights in the pub, jars of last summer's fruit, hens at the back door and something always simmering away on the stove. When we arrived, the farm was bursting with potential but also full of gaps: fallen-down sheds, tired soil, a crumbling walled garden, rooms and corners that hadn't yet found their purpose. Little by little, with each wall we repaired, each space we reimagined and each recipe we cooked, a home began to take shape. This book is the story of that home, and an invitation to shape your own.

Now that I'm in my fifties, I can look back at the different chapters of my life and see how they've all quietly led me here: years of training as a chef, opening my own restaurants, setting up a cookery school, living and cooking in Italy, France, America and Ireland. At the time, each move and each new beginning felt like its own story. Only now, standing in the kitchen at Broadspear or under the wisteria in the Walled Garden, do I see how all those threads have been weaving towards this: creating a home that brings every strand of my life together.

I have always loved designing a home; not just decorating, but thinking about how spaces make people feel, how rooms can invite you in, how a table can make everyone relax the moment they sit down. My idea of 'home' has developed with every place I've lived and every kitchen I've cooked in. The discipline and precision of my chef training, the chaos and joy of running restaurant kitchens, those lessons in seasonality and simplicity I learned in Italy, the generosity and conviviality of French tables, the boldness and ease of American entertaining, the deep-rooted sense of hospitality in Ireland… they all live in this farm. Years of designing restaurant kitchens and dining rooms taught me how spaces can make us feel: how a bar invites you to lean in, how a table layout changes the flow of conversation, how lighting, shelving and the way you reach for a pan can either support or fight you. I've used those same skills to shape Broadspear, from the layout of the Walled Garden and the pergola kitchen to The Cork Arms pub in the woods and the Pickling Shed tucked against the garden wall.

This book is part cookbook, part seasonal companion and part love letter to the art of making a place truly yours. It gathers more than one hundred and twenty new recipes, seasonal menus and stories from Broadspear, but at its heart it is about how food, spaces and rituals come together to create a happy and fulfilling life. There are one-pan suppers for busy weeks, long summer garden lunches, birthday feasts, Christmas gatherings, St Patrick's Day spreads, cocktails and canapés, all designed to be cooked and shared in a way that feels generous and unforced, the way home should.

The chapters move through the rooms and corners that have become the backbone of our forever home. In the Pickling Shed, my 'sustainability room' built against the back of the Walled Garden, I spend one day a week turning abundance into jams, pickles, chutneys, compotes and ice creams, lining the shelves with jars that carry our seasons forward. We follow spring and summer, autumn and winter through recipes and ideas for eating indoors and out: Easter lunches in the glasshouse, big garden parties in the Walled Garden, Sunday lunches in The Cork Arms pub in the woods, cosy suppers in front of the fire. Seasonal menus wind through the book, helping you to gather dishes into occasions, so you feel guided rather than overwhelmed when it's your turn to host.

The animals are part of this home-making too. Our hens, woodland pigs, Aberdeen Angus cattle, Aylesbury ducks and bees are not just livestock; they shape the land, the way we eat and the feeling of the place. Their eggs, meat and honey find their way into the recipes we cook at home, yes, but their daily presence – scratching under the fruit trees, snuffling in the woods, grazing the fields – is what makes Broadspear feel truly alive. The Walled Vegetable and Fruit Garden, with its rose-covered arches and wisteria-draped pergola kitchen at the centre, is both

pantry and sitting room for us: a place where we grow what we eat and sit right in the heart of it to cook and share meals.

Throughout the book, I open the doors to the spaces that have shaped our forever home and show how they came to be: The Cork Arms, our tiny pub in the woods built from seasoned timber and a lightning-struck tree; the glasshouse and cutting gardens; the kitchen and pantry that keep everything flowing.

I share how I design, organize and run my kitchen, the heart of our home, and how I plan the week so that cooking well, eating seasonally and entertaining sit comfortably inside a real, busy life. There are notes on building a menu that feels abundant but manageable and using what you already have – in the cupboard, the refrigerator or garden – to create something welcoming.

You do not need a farm or a walled garden or a pub in the woods to create your own forever home. You might have a single room, a balcony, a small garden, a city kitchen. What matters is your intention: paying attention to the seasons, letting your spaces reflect who you are, making room for people to gather and finding joy in the everyday acts of cooking, preserving, laying the table and lighting a candle. *Clodagh at Home* is my way of sharing how we've done that at Broadspear.

My hope is that, as you read and cook, you'll find ideas and encouragement to shape the home you dream of: one that feels deeply, unmistakably yours, and that can hold you and the people you love for years to come.

Love, Clodagh xx

The Bees

When we first arrived at Broadspear, the soil was so poor that I knew we had to heal the land before we could truly grow anything. I dreamed of vegetables, fruit trees and rows of cutting flowers, but it didn't feel right to start planting into tired earth. I wanted to begin with rejuvenation rather than extraction. That's where the bees came in...

We started with six hives. Before they arrived, we spent a day with a local beekeeper, who kitted us out in bee suits and shared all she could in one whirlwind lesson: how to approach a hive calmly, what to look for on each frame, how to tell if a colony is thriving. We were both terrified and fascinated as we were handed the keys to a whole other world that had always existed, just out of sight.

One morning, the postman turned up clutching a small box plastered with LIVE ANIMALS stickers, looking both alarmed and deeply curious. We stood in the yard as I explained that inside was our new queen. When we opened it, there she was: a tiny, regal speck in her own little cage, surrounded by attendants. The postman gave a nervous laugh that said, 'This is *not* what I signed up for on my round today!'

Eight years later, I can see what the bees have done for Broadspear. Their pollination has transformed the farm: the orchard, the vegetable beds, the cutting flowers. All of them depend on that constant, gentle traffic of bees moving from blossom to blossom.

I hadn't expected how profoundly grounding it is to work with bees. You can't rush them or bend them to your will; they set the pace. On days when the farm feels demanding or uncertain, opening a hive requires a different kind of presence: slow, attentive, calm. The low, steady hum as you lift each frame has a way of drawing you out of your own head and into theirs, into this intricate, ordered world where every bee has a role. They can fly over five miles in search of nectar before returning unerringly to the hive. When a bee discovers a rich source, she performs a small, purposeful dance that communicates direction and distance, guiding the others. It's impossible not to be in awe of such instinct.

We've learned to read their subtle signals: the temperament of the colony, the weight of the hive, the scent when the lid is lifted. There have been losses, harsh winters or difficult springs, reminding us how delicate the balance is. But those have only deepened our respect for our bees. Our first pot of honey was, without doubt, the most beautiful and meaningful spoonful I've eaten. I could taste the wild flowers, the young orchard finding its feet. We now get 100–150 pots a year, and its taste changes every season, but the undertones are citrus from the lime trees and delicate florals from the lavender.

That first spoon of honey felt like a promise, the boost I needed to carry on with what seemed an overwhelming project. Looking back, I can see that the beehives and the bees themselves were at the beginning of what Broadspear has become. They are more than pollinators or honey-makers; they are quiet teachers. They've shown us that rebuilding land is not about control, but partnership; about creating the right conditions, then trusting nature to do the rest.

19 August 2023

Archiving the tasting notes of the honey, 9 August 2021

Beehives with a view of the cedar tree beyond, 21 June 2020

Harry and I with our first honey harvest jarred! 13 Sepember 2019

Busy beekeepers, 8 June 2023

Our first honeycomb, 21 August 2019

Misty morning beyond the beehives, 14 November 2021

Our first honey harvest, 13 September 2019

Our honey jar label, 21 August 2020

The Pickling Shed

DRYING FLOWERS & HERBS

One of the simplest, most sustainable and satisfying ways to preserve the seasons in the garden. There is a quiet rhythm to this – gathering, tying, hanging – and a wonderful sense of extending the productive times into the colder months. I keep dried flowers and herbs hanging in my Pickling Shed beside our Walled Garden, which I restored and converted a couple of years ago (read more about this on page 20). I put in hooks on the rafters and under the shelves, which is where I dry flowers and herbs... it really looks so magical when you open the door.

I love to use everything we grow on the farm, and there is something deeply special about capturing beautiful flowers at their peak to enjoy long after their season has passed. I use them throughout the house, hung in loose bunches. They bring both beauty and a gentle connection back to the garden. From the cutting garden, I dry armfuls of lavender, roses, hydrangeas, statice, achillea and more delicate blooms such as cornflowers and calendula. Each holds its colour and character in its own way, creating a soft, natural palette that I love to use around my home.

I grow and dry a mixture of herbs such as mint, rosemary and thyme, which I often blend into homemade herb salts or teas (see overleaf). These make the most delicious rubs for meat, or a simple seasoning for roasted vegetables. Dill and fennel are also favourites; their delicate fronds and seeds dry beautifully and are perfect for scattering over fish or folding into spice mixes. I dry the herb flowers, too: fennel flowers, onion blossoms and other edible blooms that bring both flavour and beauty, adding colour and a gentle fragrance to dishes, salts and even table settings.

HOW TO DRY HERBS

1. Harvest on a dry morning, once the dew has lifted, choosing healthy, unblemished stems.
2. Gather into small, loose bunches and tie with kitchen twine. Hang upside down in a warm, dry, well-ventilated space, away from direct sunlight.
3. Leave for 1–2 weeks, until crisp and crumbly.
4. Strip the leaves from the stems and seal in airtight jars, then store them in a cool, dark place to preserve their flavour and colour.

HOW TO DRY FLOWERS

1. Pick on a dry day when blooms are just fully open, avoiding any damp or damaged flowers.
2. For sturdy stems, tie into small bunches and hang upside down.
3. For delicate flowers, lay flat on baking parchment-lined trays in a single layer.
4. Place in a warm, airy room away from direct sunlight. Allow to dry slowly for several days or up to a week, until papery to the touch. Store in airtight containers in a cool, dark place.

HERBAL SALTS

One of those super-handy kitchen staples that transform everything they are sprinkled on. These salts let you capture the flavour of the garden at its peak and keep it on the shelf, ready to use in an instant. A little jar of herb salt can do the work of both seasoning and herbs in one pinch: scattered over roast vegetables, rubbed on meat or fish, or sprinkled over eggs, salads and soups. They are also a wonderful way to use and preserve armfuls of herbs that might otherwise go to waste, turning them into something you can reach for every day. Once you start making your own blends, it is hard to imagine cooking without them. Plus, they look so great in a beautiful jar in your kitchen!

HERBY ROASTING SALT

MAKES 1 SMALL JAR

2 tablespoons dried rosemary leaves
2 tablespoons dried thyme leaves
1 tablespoon dried mint leaves
6 tablespoons sea salt flakes

1 Mix everything together, gently crushing the mixture between your fingers to release the herb oils. Store in a labelled airtight jar and use as a rub for meats or sprinkled over roasted vegetables.

DILLY FISH RUB

MAKES 1 SMALL JAR

6 tablespoons dried dill
3 teaspoons fennel seeds, lightly crushed
Finely grated zest of 3 lemons
Freshly ground black pepper
6 tablespoons sea salt flakes

1 Mix all the ingredients together, gently crushing the mixture between your fingers to release the dil, fennel and lemon oils. Store in a labelled airtight jar and rub over fish before roasting or grilling, or sprinkle over vegetables for a light, aromatic seasoning.

HERBAL TEAS FROM THE GARDEN

There is something wonderfully satisfying about making tea from herbs you have grown and dried yourself. Each year, I build up a little apothecary of my own tea mixtures, ready to blend into a soothing cup of chamomile for busy days, a bright lemon verbena infusion for a mid-afternoon pick-me-up, or a mint tea or fennel and dill brew for after a meal.

AFTER-SUPPER MINT TEA

MAKES A POT FOR 2

1 tablespoon dried mint leaves
A few slices of root ginger (optional)
Honey (optional)

1 Place the dried mint and ginger, if using, in a teapot. Pour over 500ml (18fl oz) of freshly boiled water and cover. Leave to infuse for 5 minutes. Strain if needed and sweeten with a little honey, if you like. Serve warm.

CALMING CHAMOMILE TEA

MAKES A POT FOR 2

1 tablespoon dried chamomile flowers
Honey, or lemon slices (optional)

1 Put the chamomile flowers in a teapot. Pour over 500ml (18fl oz) of freshly boiled water and cover. Leave to infuse for 5 minutes. Strain and serve, adding honey or a slice of lemon, whichever appeals to you most.

REFRESHING LEMON VERBENA TEA

MAKES A POT FOR 2

1 tablespoon dried lemon verbena leaves
Lemon slices (optional)

1 Place the dried verbena leaves in a teapot. Pour over 500ml (18fl oz) of freshly boiled water and cover. Leave to infuse for 5–6 minutes. Strain and serve with lemon slices, if you like, for a bright, citrus note.

DIGESTIVE BREW: FENNEL & DILL TEA

MAKES A POT FOR 2

1 teaspoon dried fennel seeds
1 tablespoon dried dill

1 Lightly crush the fennel seeds, then place in a teapot with the dried dill. Pour over 500ml (18fl oz) of freshly boiled water and cover. Leave to infuse for 5–7 minutes, then strain and serve.

TARRAGON VINEGAR

MAKES 1 × 500ML (18FL OZ) BOTTLE

So simple to make, as easy as making a pot of tea. I snip tarragon from the garden and steep it in vinegar in my Pickling Shed, where it sits on the shelf ready for whenever I need it. I love having a bottle to hand for making a quick béarnaise sauce; it brings that quintessential tangy tarragon flavour that feels so classically French. It is also beautiful whisked into a simple French-style dressing with olive oil and mustard to spoon over warm new potatoes, or drizzle over roast chicken and green beans. A small bottle goes a very long way and instantly lifts so many everyday dishes.

Handful of bushy tarragon sprigs (at least 6–8)
500ml (18fl oz) good-quality white wine vinegar, or Champagne vinegar

1. Rinse the tarragon sprigs gently under cold water, then pat completely dry with a clean tea towel or kitchen paper.
2. Lightly bruise the tarragon with the back of a knife or a wooden spoon to help release its oils.
3. Place the tarragon into a sterilized glass bottle or jar (see below). Pour over the vinegar, making sure the herbs are fully submerged.
4. Seal and store in a cool, dark place for 2–3 weeks, swirling the bottle every few days to encourage the flavours to infuse. Taste the vinegar; when the flavour is to your liking, strain it into a fresh sterilized bottle, label and seal.

How to sterilize jars & bottles

1. *Preheat the oven to 180°C fan (400°F), Gas Mark 6.*
2. *Check that the jars or bottles have no chips or cracks. Wash the jars or bottles and lids thoroughly in hot soapy water, then rinse and dry.*
3. *Line a roasting or baking tray with baking parchment. Place the clean jars or bottles and lids on the prepared tray and into the preheated oven for 10 minutes.*
4. *Allow to cool, or use warm when preserving a warm mixture.*

AUTUMN APPLE CHUTNEY

MAKES ABOUT 12 JARS

This chutney has been with me for a very long time! I've been making it for about twenty-five years, ever since my days with a stall at the farmers' markets in Ireland, and it quickly became one of those jars people would come back for time and again. It's a fabulous way to use up fallen apples in autumn, turning windfalls into something deeply spiced and comforting for the colder months. The flavour is rich and layered: sweet-sharp apple cooked down with onions, brown sugar and cider vinegar, warmed with ginger, cloves, chilli and turmeric and rounded out with a little butter. It's tangy but soft, with a gentle heat and a golden, almost caramelized depth that makes it as good with cold meats and cheese as it is with simple sausages or a slice of pork pie. The longer you leave it in the jar, the better it gets.

3kg (6lb 8oz) cooking apples, peeled, quartered and cored
80g (2¾oz) unsalted butter
3 onions, finely chopped
600g (1lb 5oz) brown sugar
12 cloves
1 tablespoon chilli powder
2 tablespoons ground turmeric
7.5cm (3-inch) piece of root ginger, peeled and grated
600ml (20fl oz) apple cider vinegar
Sea salt and freshly ground black pepper

1 Chop the apples into small chunks.

2 Place a large saucepan over a low heat and melt the butter. Then stir in the apples and onions followed by the brown sugar, cloves, chilli powder, turmeric, ginger and cider vinegar and season with salt and pepper. Mix well.

3 Cover the saucepan, increase the heat and bring to the boil, then reduce the heat and leave to simmer over a medium heat for 20 minutes, stirring every 5 minutes.

4 Take the lid off, reduce the heat to its lowest and leave to cook for 30 minutes, stirring more towards the end of cooking so it doesn't catch on the pan. The apples should have broken down and the chutney turned a rich golden brown.

5 Use the back of a wooden spoon to crush up the apples. Take the saucepan off the heat; the chutney will thicken more as it cools.

6 Once the chutney has cooled, spoon into 12 sterilized jars (see page 17), label and seal.

SALTER

The Pickling Shed

The Pickling Shed is my dream room, and it's also where I feel I'm at my most creative. It began, like The Cork Arms (see page 182), as another fallen-down shed: a small, forgotten structure tacked on to the back of the Walled Garden, right beside the gate. The back wall of the Shed is the wall of the garden itself: I often press my hands against it from inside, knowing that fruit and vegetables are growing on the other side, and I always felt that this building needed to be, in some way, directly connected to the produce.

For years it sat there slumping slowly while my attention was pulled to other parts of the farm, quietly waiting for its purpose to arrive. The idea for the Pickling Shed came out of pure necessity. At certain points in the year, we have huge abundance: vegetables, meats, herbs, fruit, flowers, eggs. It is wonderful and overwhelming all at once. I wanted a functional space where everything could be put, so nothing would get lost or go to waste – a kind of 'sustainability room', if you like – dedicated to looking after the harvest and honouring that wall that separates growing from preserving. I rebuilt the shed with that purpose in mind: walls lined with shelving for jars and bottles, beams across the ceiling for hanging and drying, counter space all the way around for equipment and a table in the centre where I can prep and experiment.

My aim is to spend one day a week in the Pickling Shed throughout the year. It's my working sanctuary. In there I pickle vegetables and make chutneys, jams, ice creams and soups, stews and so on. In the overhang beside it, where we store all our firewood, I have a double freezer ready to hold big batches of soup, stews from our beef and pork, and tubs of ice cream to feed us through the months ahead. I've slowly taught myself how to dry flowers and herbs, turning them into teas and salt rubs (see pages 12–15), and the dried flowers become my stand-ins when there are no fresh blossoms in the garden. We store our honey there, as well as the apple juice pressed from fallen apples, and trays of eggs that wait to be turned into pasta or ice cream. Some of my favourite days in the Pickling Shed are when we have a big harvest of something particularly fragrant, such as lavender. That's when I feel most creative. I love experimenting with all the different things I can make from it: lavender oil for baths, lavender water spray for linens, and last year, big batches of lavender ice cream made with our fresh eggs and sweetened with honey from our beehives (for the recipe, see page 32).

Magic happens in the Pickling Shed when I take different produce from around the farm and bring it together, testing new combinations and seeing what they become. I'm always pushing myself to be creative about how to preserve different vegetables and fruits in many ways – pickled, dried, fermented, churned into ice cream, cooked into jam – so that every harvest finds its perfect form and that garden wall feels properly honoured. It is genuinely magical in the Pickling Shed when you open the door. From the outside, people expect a simple store room; inside, it's the heart of our farm. Dried flowers and herbs hang from the ceiling and across the beams, jars glow with jewel-coloured pickles, jams and syrups, and the shelves are crowded with bottles and boxes of things we've made. I love bringing friends and family in there and asking them to choose whatever they like from the shelves: a jar of pickles, a bag of dried fruit, a bottle of apple juice, a tub of lavender ice cream. The memories created within those jars are as precious as the contents themselves. It feels a little like opening a bottle of wine: you're not just tasting the liquid, you're uncorking a moment in time. Nothing is lost, because I've preserved it.

The Pickling Shed, August 2024

Plum harvest, August 2025

Greengages, August 2023

Lavender harvest, 23 July 2025

Making lavendar bath oil, 28 July 2025

Basil pesto! June 2023

Strawberry & Geranium Cordial (see page 35), June 2024

Rhubarb vodka! 29 June 2021

Strawberry and lemon ice cream, 26 June 2024

QUICK PICKLING BRINE

ENOUGH FOR ABOUT 500G (1LB 2OZ) OF VEG

Quick pickling has become one of my weekend rituals, as I adore the contrast of a sweet, sharp vinaigrette against the bright, crunchy bite of just-picked vegetables. It's the perfect solution when you have vegetables on the brink of going soft, giving them a delicious new lease of life.

200ml (7fl oz) apple cider vinegar, or white wine vinegar
2 tablespoons caster sugar (about 25g / 1oz)
1 tablespoon fine sea salt (about 15g / ½oz)

Optional aromatics
1 teaspoon mustard seeds
½ teaspoon black peppercorns
A few dill, thyme or parsley sprigs
1–2 garlic cloves, sliced

1 Prepare the veg: slice any cucumbers and courgettes into coins or ribbons; cut carrots into thin batons; cook beetroot until tender, then slice or wedge the spheres. Pack the vegetables tightly into a sterilized jar (see page 17), tucking in any aromatics.

2 Pour the vinegar, sugar and salt into a small saucepan and add 200ml (7fl oz) of water. Bring just to the boil, stirring to dissolve the sugar and salt.

3 Pour the hot brine over the veg to fully submerge. Tap the jar gently to release air bubbles, and top up with more brine if needed. (Just make a little more in exactly the same way.)

4 Allow it to cool to room temperature, then chill. They're tasty after 30–60 minutes, better after a few hours, and keep in the refrigerator for 1–2 weeks.

PICKLED BEETS with dill & mustard seeds

MAKES ABOUT 2 × 300G (10½OZ) JARS

I always have a big stock of pickled beets to last throughout the year stored in the Pickling Shed, as they are so fabulous to pop in the centre of the table for lunches or light suppers, to add to salads, a roast chicken, or accompany an omelette or soft cheeses. On the farm we grow a mix of varieties – deep red, golden and rainbow – and I love how their colours are captured in the jar. Here, the sweetness of the beets is lifted with a gentle, aromatic dill brine with warming mustard seeds, which tastes especially good alongside smoked fish, cold meats or simply tucked into a salad. It's a simple way of bottling the harvest and the jars look so vibrant on the shelves.

6 small beetroot, trimmed and scrubbed
4 dill sprigs, cut into 2-3cm (1-inch) pieces
160ml (5½fl oz) white wine vinegar
140g (5oz) caster sugar
1 teaspoon mustard seeds
½ teaspoon black peppercorns
1 teaspoon salt

1. Place the beetroot in a saucepan and cover with cold water. Bring to the boil over a medium heat and cook for about 30 minutes, until tender. To test, gently push back the skin of a beetroot: if it slips off easily, it is cooked. Drain and refresh under cold water.
2. Put the dill, vinegar, sugar, mustard seeds, peppercorns, salt and 150ml (¼ pint) of cold water in a small saucepan and set over a medium heat. Stir for 2-3 minutes, until the sugar has dissolved and the mixture comes just up to a simmer.
3. Peel the beetroot using a small sharp knife, then cut into small wedges. Pack these into warm, sterilized jars (see page 17).
4. Pour the hot vinegar mixture over the beetroot, making sure the wedges are completely covered. Allow to cool completely, then label, seal and store in a cool, dark place.

Storage Note

Stored in a cool, dark place or the refrigerator, the pickled beets will keep for up to 3 months. Once opened, keep refrigerated, making sure the beets are covered with brine, and enjoy within 2–3 weeks.

BLACKBERRY JAM
with a hint of lemon

MAKES ABOUT 8 × 250G (9OZ) JARS

There is something timeless about blackberry season on the farm, when the lanes and hedgerows turn dark with fruit and life slows just enough for picking. Harry heads out with a basket and comes back with it stained deep purple, the blackberries still warm from the sun. In the Pickling Shed, the berries are tumbled into a pot with lemon and sugar. This is the kind of jam that feels rooted in place and season, made simply to use what the land gives us. A bright hint of lemon lifts the rich, inky berries and every jar feels like a little store of late-summer sunshine in the darker months. Served on my Clodagh's Soda bread (see page 122), toasted and spread with salted butter, heaven...

1kg (2lb 4oz) blackberries
Finely grated zest and juice of 2 lemons
1kg (2lb 4oz) jam sugar

1. Place the blackberries, lemon zest and juice in a large saucepan, preserving pan or casserole dish and simmer gently for about 15 minutes until the fruit is soft.
2. Meanwhile, warm the sugar in a heatproof bowl in a low oven. When the fruit is cooked, add the warmed sugar and stir over a low heat until it has dissolved.
3. Increase the heat and bring to the boil, then cook at a rolling boil for 10–15 minutes until setting point has been reached (see below).
4. Once the jam is at setting point, take the pan off the heat, spoon any foam off the top and leave it to sit for about 10 minutes. Ladle the hot jam into warm, sterilized jars (see page 17) and seal. Leave to cool completely, then label and store in a cool, dark place.

Storage Note

Stored in a cool, dark place, the jam will keep for up to 1 year. Once opened, keep in the refrigerator and enjoy within 1 month.

Testing for a Set

Place a saucer in the freezer for 10 minutes so that it is chilled. Remove from the freezer and place 1 teaspoon of the jam on the chilled saucer. Push the jam with your finger: if it wrinkles, it is set.

BROADSPEAR
BROADSPEAR
BROADSPEAR
BROADSPEAR

STRAWBERRY & SWEET GERANIUM JAM

MAKES ABOUT 3 × 300G (10½OZ) JARS

Every summer at Broadspear there comes a moment when the strawberries all seem to ripen at once, and the kitchen is suddenly full of bowls, trays and colanders brimming over with bright red fruit. It's the happiest kind of glut and I always transform a generous share of it into this jam, to keep that brief, perfect season going a little longer. Here, I tuck in sweet geranium leaves as the strawberries cook; they lend a soft, floral perfume that sits just behind the fruit, like a whisper of rose and citrus. The berries collapse into a glossy, ruby-red preserve that is everything you want strawberry jam to be: bright, sweet and full of flavour. There is nothing more delicious than spooning it on a freshly baked scone with a thick layer of clotted cream, or salty Irish butter, or both!

1kg (2lb 4oz) strawberries
400g (14oz) jam sugar
2 tablespoons honey
12 scented geranium leaves, such as rose or lemon
1 lemon, sliced

1 Place the strawberries, sugar and honey in a large saucepan, preserving pan or flameproof casserole. Swish the strawberries into the sugar using a potato masher, leaving a few chunky bits in there to add a little texture. Stir in the sweet geranium leaves and lemon slices.
2 Place the pan over a medium heat, bring it to the boil, stirring as you do, then increase the heat and cook at a rolling boil for about 10 minutes until setting point has been reached (see page 25). Turn the heat off, carefully skim any foam off the top, remove the lemon slices and geranium leaves,then leave to settle for about 10 minutes.
3 Divide between warm sterilized jars (see page 17), then seal. Leave to cool completely, then label and store in a cool, dark place.

Storage Note

Stored in a cool, dark place, the jam will keep for up to 1 year. Once opened, keep in the refrigerator and enjoy within 1 month.

FIG, THYME & ORANGE JAM

MAKES ABOUT 3 × 250G (9OZ) JARS

When we first arrived at Broadspear, there was very little growing in the way of fruit. There were a few apple trees and one fig, but the figs would begin to form, then dry up and fall before they had ripened. We pruned it back, cared for it well and made sure it was deeply watered through the hot summer. Now, each year, it gives us an abundance of beautiful fresh figs. I have taken clippings from that tree and now have more fig plants growing in pots in the glasshouse. This jam is one of my favourite ways to use them, especially served with blue cheeses such as Gorgonzola, or alongside a good mature Cheddar. In this recipe, the sweetness of the figs is balanced by orange and thyme.

600g (1lb 5oz) fresh figs, stalks removed, roughly chopped
Finely grated zest and juice of 1 orange
600g (1lb 5oz) jam sugar
4 thyme sprigs

1. Place the figs, orange zest and juice, sugar and thyme in a large saucepan, preserving pan or casserole dish with 200ml (7fl oz) of water. Stir together and set over a medium-high heat.
2. Bring to the boil, stirring until the sugar completely dissolves. Reduce the heat and simmer gently for 45–60 minutes, stirring occasionally, until the jam is thickened and glossy.
3. Remove the thyme sprigs and test for setting point (see page 25). Skim off any foam, allow to settle for 10 minutes, then ladle the hot jam into warm, sterilized jars (see page 17) and seal. Leave to cool completely, then label and store in a cool, dark place.

Storage Note

Stored in a cool, dark place, the jam will keep for up to 1 year. Once opened, keep in the refrigerator and enjoy within 1 month.

BROADSPEAR PLUM JAM

MAKES ABOUT 6 × 250G (9OZ) JARS

There are three plum trees in our orchard at Broadspear, a birthday present from Harry five years ago, and this past summer they were more generous than ever. Harry picked more than 25kg (55lb) of fruit, and the branches kept on giving all season. The variety we have is called Warwickshire Drooper, a beautiful plum that tastes almost like an apricot: sweet, fragrant and perfect for preserving. This jam is one of my favourite ways to use the harvest; I add plenty of our own honey, a little sugar and lemon to brighten everything, and the resulting flavour reminds me of a classic apricot jam. With the glut of plums, I make jams and pies, and freeze halved, pitted fruit so it doesn't turn bitter, but it's these jars of jam lined up on the shelf that feel like the truest taste of our plum season.

1kg (2lb 4oz) plums, halved and pitted
600g (1lb 5oz) jam sugar
2 tablespoons honey
Finely grated zest and juice of 1 lemon

1. Place the plums and 300ml (½ pint) of water in a large saucepan, preserving pan or flameproof casserole. Bring to the boil, then reduce the heat and simmer for 10 minutes, until the fruit has softened and begun to break down.
2. Stir in the sugar, honey, lemon zest and juice and keep stirring over a low heat until the sugar has completely dissolved.
3. Increase the heat and bring the jam up to a rolling boil. Keep it at the boil for about 10 minutes, stirring every few minutes, until it begins to thicken and reach setting point (see page 25).
4. Skim off any foam that rises to the surface, then remove from the heat and leave the jam to rest for 10 minutes so the fruit settles.
5. Using a ladle or jug, pour the hot jam into warm, sterilized jars (see page 17) and seal. Leave to cool completely, then label and store in a cool, dark place.

Storage Note

Stored in a cool, dark place, the jam will keep for up to 1 year. Once opened, keep in the refrigerator and eat within 1 month.

B

LAVENDER & HONEY ICE CREAM

MAKES ABOUT 600ML (20FL OZ)

The first thing you'll notice when you come to Broadspear is lavender... I have a bit of an obsession with it. There are hundreds of bushes threaded through the borders and around the farm, at first planted to help keep the deer away from the garden beds and now very much part of the place.

Last year, I invested in an ice cream machine, one of the best things I've ever done, and this was the first ice cream I made in it. Using our own lavender and honey made it feel special. The perfume of the lavender here is soft and floral rather than soapy, and it gently lingers as you eat. It is summer at our farm in one spoonful.

350ml (12fl oz) whole milk
250ml (9fl oz) double cream
200g (7oz) clear honey
1 tablespoon vanilla extract
7 tablespoons fresh lavender flowers, plus more (optional) to serve
6 egg yolks
150g (5½oz) golden caster sugar

1. Pour the milk, cream, honey, vanilla and 5 tablespoons of the lavender flowers into a large saucepan. Place over a medium heat and slowly bring just to the boil, stirring occasionally, then reduce the heat to low and let it sit for a couple of minutes to infuse.
2. Meanwhile, whisk the egg yolks and sugar together in a large bowl until slightly thickened and paler. Slowly pour the warm milk mixture into the eggs, whisking constantly. Once combined, return the mixture to the saucepan.
3. Cook over a medium-low heat, stirring all the time, until it thickens slightly and coats the back of the spoon. Do not let it boil.
4. Strain the custard through a fine sieve into a clean bowl to remove the lavender (and any lumps). Stir in the remaining 2 tablespoons of lavender flowers, then leave to cool completely. Cover and chill in the refrigerator until very cold.
5. Churn the cold custard in an ice cream machine according to the manufacturer's instructions, then transfer to a freezable container and freeze until firm. If you don't have a machine, pour into a shallow freezable container and freeze for 3–4 hours, stirring every 30–40 minutes to break up ice crystals.
6. Serve scoops of ice cream with a few lavender flowers scattered over the top, if you can, as it looks so pretty!

ELDERFLOWER CORDIAL

MAKES ABOUT 2 LITRES (3½ PINTS)

At the farm, we have a large elderflower bush that bursts into frothy white blossom at the start of summer, just as the days begin to stretch out and warm up. I love gathering the flowers on a dry morning, when they are fragrant and open, and turning them into this simple cordial: it feels like bottling the scent of early summer. We drink it with still or sparkling water, or turn it into a light elderflower cocktail with prosecco or Champagne. It is also beautiful in jellies, sorbets and ice creams, adding a gentle floral note that feels very special.

30 heads of elderflower
3 lemons
1kg (2lb 4oz) caster sugar
2 teaspoons citric acid (optional; helps preserve the cordial for up to a month)

1. Gently shake and rinse the elderflower heads to remove any insects, then remove the blossoms from the stalks and place them in a large heatproof bowl or saucepan. Finely grate the lemon zest over the elderflowers, then slice the zested lemons and add the slices to the bowl or pan.
2. Put the caster sugar and 2 litres (3½ pints) of water into a separate saucepan and bring to the boil, stirring to dissolve the sugar. Once it reaches the boil, remove from the heat and allow the syrup to cool slightly.
3. Pour the warm syrup over the elderflowers and lemons, then stir in the citric acid, if using. Cover the bowl with a clean cloth and leave to infuse in the refrigerator (or a cool place) for 24 hours.
4. The next day, strain the cordial through a sieve lined with muslin into a jug, then funnel into sterilized glass bottles (see page 17). Seal, label and store in the refrigerator.
5. To use the cordial, just mix 1 part cordial with 2 parts water for a refreshing drink. Or, for a sparkling elderflower cocktail, fill a Champagne flute with 1 part cordial and 2 parts prosecco or Champagne.

Storage Note

Stored in the refrigerator, the cordial will keep for up to 3–4 weeks. Once opened, keep chilled and enjoy within a couple of weeks.

STRAWBERRY & GERANIUM CORDIAL

MAKES ABOUT 300ML (½ PINT)

As you will already know (see page 27), I adore the combination of fragrant geranium and sweet strawberry, which works brilliantly as a cordial. This recipe is just as delicious later in the season with raspberries or blackberries, too. It's wonderful simply mixed with water, but I especially love turning it into a sparkling, refreshing drink: 100ml (3½fl oz) cordial topped up with 900ml (1½ pints) sparkling water, a few mint sprigs and a sliced lemon, served over ice. The cordial also doubles as a beautiful syrup for drizzling over ice cream, stirring into cake batters, or brushing on sponge layers for extra flavour and moisture: a little bottle of summer that goes a very long way. And just think of the fabulous hot-weather cocktails you could make with it!

400g (14oz) strawberries, hulled
200g (7oz) granulated sugar
6 scented geranium leaves, such as rose or lemon (optional)

1. Place the strawberries, sugar, 200ml (7fl oz) of water and the geranium leaves, if using, in a large saucepan. Set over a medium heat and bring to a gentle simmer, stirring until the sugar has dissolved.
2. Simmer for about 10 minutes, until the strawberries are very soft and the liquid has become deep red and fragrant.
3. Remove from the heat and carefully blend with a stick blender until smooth (take care: it's hot). Leave to cool completely.
4. Strain through a sieve lined with muslin into a jug, then funnel into a sterilized bottle (see page 17), seal and label.
5. Store in the refrigerator and use within 2 weeks.

Spring & Summer

HOMEMADE TAGLIOLINI with butter, broad beans & Parmesan

SERVES 2

Some of my favourite evenings at Broadspear are when I roll out homemade tagliolini and finish it with whatever is perfect that week in the garden. This simple bowl of pasta is all about that moment when the beans are sweet and tender. When broad beans are out of season, peas are just as delicious here, bringing the same bright sweetness. The sauce is nothing more than good butter, starchy pasta-cooking water and a handful of cheese, shaken together until it turns silky and coats the tagliolini strands.

150–180g (5½–6oz) podded broad beans (from 500–600g/1lb 2oz–1lb 5oz beans in the pod)
200g (7oz) fresh tagliolini (for homemade, see page 126)
40g (1½oz) unsalted butter
2 tablespoons extra virgin olive oil, plus more to serve
50g (1¾oz) finely grated Parmesan, plus more to serve
Small handful of flat leaf parsley leaves, finely chopped
Squeeze of lemon juice
Sea salt flakes and freshly ground black pepper

1. Bring a large saucepan of well-salted water to the boil. Add the podded broad beans and blanch for 2–3 minutes, until just tender and bright green. Drain with a slotted spoon, reserving the water for the pasta. If the beans are large, slip them from their skins.
2. In the same saucepan of boiling water, cook the fresh tagliolini for 2–3 minutes, or until just al dente. Reserve a mug of the starchy pasta-cooking water, then drain.
3. While the pasta cooks, gently melt the butter with the olive oil in a wide frying pan over a medium heat. Add the broad beans with a pinch of salt and warm through for 1–2 minutes.
4. Tip the hot, just-drained tagliolini straight into the pan with the buttery beans. Toss everything together over a low heat, adding a splash or so of the reserved pasta-cooking water to create a light, glossy emulsion.
5. Take the pan off the heat and add the grated Parmesan and parsley. Toss again, loosening with a little more pasta-cooking water if needed, until the pasta is lightly coated and silky. Taste and season with salt, pepper and a small squeeze of lemon juice.
6. Divide between 2 warmed bowls, finishing with a little more Parmesan and a drizzle of olive oil.

SUMMER GARDEN GAZPACHO with tomato, cucumber & mint

SERVES 6 AS A STARTER

When our glasshouse tomatoes finally all ripen at once, this is the recipe I reach for. All those different heritage varieties – from chocolate cherries to deep crimson beefsteaks to sweet little Sungolds – are blended into a chilled gazpacho that tastes of pure summer. I finish it with a bright, crunchy summer garden mixture made from whatever is spilling out of the beds: cucumbers, peppers, herbs and a little red onion. It's vibrant, make-ahead and perfect for pouring into chilled bowls or glasses for easy entertaining: a delicious way to celebrate the glut.

1kg (2lb 4oz) very ripe tomatoes, chopped
100g (3½oz) slightly stale crusty white or sourdough bread, torn into pieces
2 red peppers, deseeded and chopped
1 cucumber, chopped
2 spring onions, chopped
2 garlic cloves, finely grated or crushed
3–4 tablespoons sherry vinegar, to taste
Small handful of mint leaves, chopped
200ml (7fl oz) extra virgin olive oil
Sea salt flakes and freshly ground black pepper

For the topping

½ cucumber, finely chopped
2 tomatoes, finely chopped
½ red onion, finely chopped
1 red pepper, deseeded and finely chopped
1 tablespoon torn basil leaves
1 tablespoon very fruity extra virgin olive oil, plus more to serve
Splash of sherry vinegar

1 Place the tomatoes, bread, red peppers, cucumber, spring onions, garlic, 3 tablespoons of the sherry vinegar and most of the chopped mint in a blender or food processor. Season generously with salt and pepper and blend until completely smooth.

2 With the motor still running, stream in the olive oil to emulsify it into the soup. This gives a creamy, almost velvety texture. Taste and add a little more vinegar, salt and pepper, if you want.

3 Pour the gazpacho through a fine sieve set over a large bowl or jug, using the back of a ladle or spoon to press the liquid through. Discard the solids left in the sieve. Cover and chill in the refrigerator for at least 1 hour, or until very cold, along with some serving bowls or glasses.

4 Meanwhile, in a bowl, mix the topping ingredients together and season with salt and pepper. Toss together and set aside for at least 15 minutes, so the flavours mingle.

5 When ready to serve, give the gazpacho a stir and check the seasoning once more. Pour into the chilled bowls or glasses and spoon some of the topping over. Finish with a final drizzle of very fruity olive oil, a pinch of sea salt flakes and the reserved mint. Serve straight away.

SIMPLE BROAD BEANS with herbs & pecorino

SERVES 2 AS A SIDE DISH OR STARTER

I will be honest: I wasn't *that* excited planting out our first broad beans. My memories of broad beans were, well, grey. And slightly bitter. But – oh my goodness – the first taste of a freshly grown broad bean and I was gobsmacked at how delicious they can be. We now sit on the edge of the veg beds and eat them like sweets! Plus, they are very easy to grow (win, win).

This simple plate lets that sweetness shine. The beans are briefly blanched, then tossed with good olive oil, a squeeze of lemon juice, soft herbs and plenty of sharp pecorino. It's spring on a plate: light, fresh and joyful. I love to serve the bean mixture as a simple starter, too, with good bread, spooned over ricotta-topped toast, or alongside grilled lamb or chicken for an easy spring supper.

Later in the season, when the beans are larger, slip them from their skins after blanching. Toss the double-podded beans with a little finely grated garlic along with the lemon zest and juice, before finishing with the pecorino, for a deeper, more savoury version.

400g (14oz) broad beans in the pod (or 150–200g / 5½–7oz podded beans)
2 tablespoons extra virgin olive oil, plus more to serve
Finely grated zest and juice of 1 lemon
Small handful of soft herb leaves (mint, flat leaf parsley or chives), finely chopped
20–30g (¾–1oz) pecorino, shaved or finely grated
Sea salt flakes and freshly ground black pepper

1. Pod the broad beans. If they are large, you can double-pod them after blanching (see page 39), but the tiny early beans are perfect as they are.
2. Bring a small saucepan of salted water to the boil. Add the beans and blanch them for 2–3 minutes, until just tender and bright green. Drain and refresh briefly under cold water, then drain again.
3. Tip the beans into a bowl and toss with the olive oil, lemon zest and juice, most of the herbs and a little salt and pepper.
4. Transfer to a shallow plate, scatter over the pecorino and the last of the herbs, then finish with a final drizzle of olive oil.

SUMMER TOMATO SALAD with herbs & balsamic vinaigrette

SERVES 4

In late summer, when the glasshouse is full of ripe tomatoes, this is the salad I make on repeat. I slice the tomatoes and fan them out on a big platter, then dress them with a simple balsamic vinaigrette that pools in all the little gaps and mingles with the juices. A handful of soft herbs from the garden – basil, parsley, chives, whatever is closest to hand – is scattered over the top. Serve this with good crusty sourdough bread for mopping up the juices, alongside grilled fish or chicken, or with burrata or mozzarella for a simple summer lunch. It's effortless, pretty and endlessly useful.

700–800g (1lb 9oz–1lb 12oz) ripe tomatoes (ideally a mix of colours and sizes), sliced
Small handful of basil leaves
Small handful of other soft herb leaves and flowers, if available (such as flat leaf parsley, chives, tarragon or oregano), finely chopped

For the vinaigrette
3 tablespoons extra virgin olive oil, plus more to serve
1 tablespoon good balsamic vinegar
1 teaspoon Dijon mustard
½ small garlic clove, finely grated or crushed (optional)
1 teaspoon clear honey
Sea salt flakes and freshly ground black pepper

1. Make the vinaigrette: in a small bowl or jar, whisk together the oil, balsamic, Dijon, garlic, if using, and honey. Season with salt and pepper to taste.
2. Arrange the tomato slices on a large platter. Sprinkle lightly with sea salt flakes and let them sit for 5–10 minutes so they start to release their juices.
3. Just before serving, spoon the balsamic vinaigrette evenly over the tomatoes. Scatter over the basil leaves and other soft herbs and flowers, if using, then finish with a little black pepper and a final drizzle of olive oil.

ASPARAGUS WITH SOFT EGG & LEMONY PANGRATTATO

SERVES 2

One of my favourite spring suppers for two. When the asparagus spears are at their sweetest, I like to keep everything simple and let them shine. The eggs are boiled just until the yolks turn silky and spoonable, then scattered with a hot, zesty pangrattato made with lemon, garlic and good olive oil. It's light but satisfying, and we love having it with a glass of cold white wine at the kitchen table on a weeknight.

The pangrattato is near-endlessly versatile; I also love it sprinkled over pasta (see page 167).

4 large eggs
300–350g (10½–12oz) asparagus (about 12 spears), woody ends snapped off
Sea salt flakes and freshly ground black pepper

For the pangrattato
2 tablespoons extra virgin olive oil, plus more to serve
½ garlic clove, finely grated or crushed
40g (1½oz) fresh coarse breadcrumbs, from sourdough or country bread
Finely grated zest of ½ lemon
1 tablespoon finely chopped flat leaf parsley leaves (optional)

1. Bring a saucepan of salted water to the boil. Gently lower in the eggs and cook them for 6 minutes for soft, jammy yolks. Lift out into a bowl of cold water and leave to cool slightly.
2. Top up the water in the saucepan, if needed, and return to the boil. Add the asparagus and cook for 2–3 minutes, until bright green and just tender. Drain well and keep warm.
3. While the eggs and asparagus cook, make the pangrattato. Warm the olive oil in a small frying pan over a medium heat. Add the garlic and breadcrumbs with a pinch of salt and cook, stirring, for 3–4 minutes until crisp and golden. Take the pan off the heat and stir in the lemon zest and parsley, if using.
4. Peel the eggs carefully and slice each in half. Arrange the asparagus on 2 warmed plates. Nestle the egg halves on top, season lightly with salt and pepper, then spoon over the hot lemony pangrattato.
5. Finish with a drizzle of extra virgin olive oil and a sprinkling of sea salt flakes.

SPRING PEA 'GUACAMOLE' WITH RADISHES

SERVES 4 AS A NIBBLE

My favourite way to make a seasonal and sustainable guac without using avocados. Sweet spring peas are blitzed with crème fraîche, lime, mint and a little chilli until bright green and creamy, then served with crisp radishes for scooping. It has all the freshness, tang and richness you want from a guacamole-style dip, but relies on ingredients that are in season here and easy to grow. A beautiful little bowl to set out and share before a spring or summer supper.

200g (7oz) peas (fresh or frozen)
2 tablespoons crème fraîche, or Greek yogurt
2 tablespoons finely chopped mint leaves, plus more (optional) to serve
½ teaspoon chilli flakes, plus more (optional) to serve
Finely grated zest and juice of 1 lime
2–3 tablespoons extra virgin olive oil, plus more to serve
Sea salt flakes and freshly ground black pepper
12 radishes, to serve

1. Cook the peas in a saucepan of boiling water for 2–3 minutes until just tender, then drain and refresh briefly under cold water.
2. Tip the peas into a food processor with the crème fraîche, mint, chilli, lime zest and juice and 2 tablespoons of the olive oil. Season with salt and pepper.
3. Pulse-blend until you have a chunky or smooth dip, as you prefer, adding a little more olive oil if needed, to loosen.
4. Spoon into a bowl, drizzle with a little more olive oil and scatter with a pinch more chilli or mint, if you like. Serve with the radishes alongside for dipping.

COURGETTE FLOWERS FILLED WITH RICOTTA & HONEY

SERVES 2

When the courgette flowers open wide in the warmth of the day, I can never resist picking a few for this simple, very special treat. We never have many in the veg garden – just a handful at a time – so these ricotta-filled blossoms feel like a little luxury. I stir honey and mint into ricotta, then spoon it into the flowers and cook them until delicate and crisp at the edges, before drizzling over more of our own honey from the beehives. I love to serve them with pea shoots, which are usually ready at the same time: their fresh, sweet crunch and tangle of green tendrils taste as bright as they look on the plate.

80g (2¾oz) ricotta
1 tablespoon finely chopped mint leaves
40g (1½oz) clear honey, plus more to serve
4 courgette flowers
200ml (7fl oz) vegetable oil
Large handful of pea shoots
Sea salt flakes

For the batter
100g (3½oz) plain flour
1 teaspoon bicarbonate of soda
About 200ml (7fl oz) soda water

1. For the filling, mix the ricotta in a bowl until soft and smooth, then stir in the mint and honey. Carefully scoop the filling into the courgette flowers: you should get 2–4 teaspoons in each, depending on size. Twist the petals gently to enclose the mix.
2. Heat the oil in a deep saucepan over a medium-high heat. Don't leave the kitchen once the oil is on the stove, as a precaution.
3. Just before you're ready to cook, prepare the batter. Sift the flour and bicarbonate of soda into a bowl. Whisk in the soda water gradually, until you have a batter the thickness of single cream. Be careful not to over-mix and don't worry if there are a few lumps.
4. Dip a stuffed courgette flower into the batter and immediately lower it into the hot oil. Repeat with a couple more; if you're scaling up the recipe, do not cook more than 3–4 at a time, so the oil stays hot enough to give a good crispy result. Cook for 1–2 minutes, until puffed up, crisp and golden brown. Drain on a plate lined with kitchen paper and sprinkle with sea salt flakes while you cook any remaining flowers.
5. Arrange the courgette flowers on a plate, sprinkle with pea shoots and drizzle with honey.

The Walled Vegetable & Fruit Garden

This was the first big project we took on when we moved to Broadspear in 2018, and at the time it felt completely overwhelming. The walls themselves were smothered in black, dead ivy that seemed almost glued to the old brick, as if it had been strangling the garden for decades. Nothing was growing there: just a big mound of earth slumped in the middle, and along one length there was simply no wall at all... perhaps there had never been one. It felt more like a forgotten enclosure than a garden, but even then, I could see the bones of something extraordinary.

We started slowly, with the walls. At weekends we would go out with forks and gently prise the dead ivy from the three-hundred-year-old brick, letting the walls breathe and heal themselves. It was painstaking work, but as the ivy came away, the character of the old garden began to emerge: warm, weathered brick that had once held heat for fruit and flowers. Then we turned our attention to the soil, which was in such poor condition we could barely plant anything in it. We rotated and turned every inch, adding organic matter again and again until it began to feel alive rather than compacted and tired.

Only once the area was cleaned up and the earth was improving did I let myself start drawing up plans. I knew I wanted to design and create a traditional walled garden with raised beds, so we could control the soil and start growing straight away, but I also wanted the garden to be somewhere we could sit and live in, not just work in. I sketched out ten raised beds arranged around a central axis, and in the middle, a pergola structure where we could create a cooking, eating and seating area. The idea was to be right in the heart of it all, to sit beneath the pergola and feel surrounded on every side by vegetables and fruit growing.

We planted mature wisteria around the posts and have nurtured it over the years; now the pergola is completely saturated in wisteria, creating a dappled, scented shade that feels like a green room at the centre of the Walled Garden. Along the open length where the wall was missing, we commissioned a local ironmonger to build a traditional fence to define the boundary and echo the age of the bricks. Year by year, as we could afford it, we added archways between the ends of the beds, gradually creating a tunnel that leads up towards the pergola. Harry planted climbing roses at the base of each arch, and now they have grown to completely cover the structures. In summer, you walk through a tunnel of roses, petals brushing your shoulders, as you make your way up to the wisteria-shaded pergola.

A few years on, we added a glasshouse, which transformed what we could grow. Inside, we have tomatoes trained along wires, vines curling overhead, chillies and figs ripening in the warmth, and citrus fruits that would never manage outside in our climate. Around the garden we planted apple and pear trees that are circled with lavender, while against the south-facing wall we've planted all our soft fruits – currants, gooseberries, raspberries – so they can soak up every drop of heat the bricks hold. Now, at any given time, the Walled Garden holds a huge variety of vegetables and fruits in different stages of growth. There are neat rows and wild tangles, blossom and tendrils, roots and leaves, all contained within those old walls that once felt so suffocated. It has become the beating, productive heart of Broadspear, a place where we grow what feeds us, sit and eat among it, and feel the full cycle of the seasons turning all around.

The first summer in our Walled Garden, 10 July 2020

The wildflower meadow in front of the Walled Garden, 12 July 2023

Wonky carrots, 21 July 2025

The eve of my wedding day, 13 August 2021

Summer table under the pergola

Summer 2023

Very pleased at the harvest of our first sweetcorn, 21 August 2021

Summer 2022

My first time growing courgettes, July 2021

SPRING RICOTTA TART with peas, asparagus & mint

SERVES 4–6

Late spring at our farm on a plate: a light, creamy ricotta filling folded with peas, asparagus and plenty of mint. It's lovely at room temperature with a radish and rocket salad, for easy lunches, picnics or relaxed suppers. Leftovers make a good lunch with a squeeze of lemon.

For the pastry

200g (7oz) plain flour, plus more to dust
100g (3½oz) unsalted butter, chilled and chopped
1 egg yolk
2–3 tablespoons cold water
Sea salt

For the filling

100g (3½oz) asparagus, cut into 2–3cm (1-inch) pieces, plus more (optional) to decorate
200g (7oz) ricotta
100ml (3½fl oz) double cream
3 eggs
200g (7oz) peas (fresh, or frozen and defrosted)
60g (2¼oz) finely grated Parmesan, or vegetarian hard cheese
3 tablespoons finely chopped mint leaves
2 spring onions, finely sliced (optional)
Freshly ground black pepper
A little olive oil

1 To make the pastry, put the flour, butter and a pinch of salt into a bowl and rub together with your fingertips until it resembles crumbs. Add the egg yolk and enough cold water to bring it together into a soft dough. Shape into a disc, wrap and chill for 30 minutes.

2 Roll out the pastry on a floured surface and use it to line a 22–24cm (8½–9½ inch) fluted loose-bottomed tart tin. Trim the edges, prick the base with a fork and chill for 10 minutes.

3 Preheat the oven to 180°C fan (400°F), Gas Mark 6. Line the pastry with baking parchment and fill with baking beans or rice. Blind-bake for 15 minutes, then remove the beans or rice and the parchment and bake for a further 5–8 minutes, until dry and lightly golden. Reduce the oven temperature to 160°C fan (350°F), Gas Mark 4.

4 While the pastry bakes, blanch the asparagus pieces in boiling salted water for 1–2 minutes until just tender and bright green. Drain, refresh briefly under cold water and pat dry.

5 For the filling, whisk together the ricotta, cream and eggs until smooth. Stir in the peas, Parmesan, asparagus, mint and spring onions, if using. Season well with salt and pepper.

6 Pour the filling into the tart case and smooth the top. Brush the pastry rim lightly with olive oil. If you like, lay a few asparagus tips on top for decoration. Bake for 25–30 minutes, or until just set with a slight wobble in the centre and lightly golden on top. Leave to cool in the tin for at least 15 minutes, then serve warm or at room temperature.

TROPÉZIENNE with raspberries

SERVES 8–10

I first tasted this – appropriately enough – in Saint-Tropez, where it was created, and ever since it has been one of my favourite bakes, with its perfectly spongey brioche and decadent syrup. So much so, that it became my mission to learn how to make it! My version is layered with vanilla cream and sweet raspberries from the garden, and has become my birthday cake.

For the brioche

250g (9oz) strong white bread flour, plus more to dust

40g (1½oz) caster sugar

½ teaspoon fine sea salt

7g (¼oz) fast-action dried yeast

3 eggs, at room temperature

60ml (4 tablespoons) whole milk, lukewarm, plus more to brush

1 teaspoon vanilla extract

120g (4¼oz) unsalted butter, very soft, plus more for the bowl and the tin

1-2 tablespoons pearl sugar, or flaked almonds

For the syrup

60g (2¼oz) caster sugar

1 teaspoon vanilla extract, or 1 tablespoon orange blossom water

For the filling

250ml (9fl oz) whole milk

1 teaspoon vanilla extract

3 large egg yolks

60g (2¼oz) caster sugar

20g (¾oz) cornflour

150ml (¼ pint) double cream

1-2 tablespoons icing sugar, to taste, plus more to dust

To finish

150-200g (5½-7oz) raspberries

1 Place the flour, sugar, salt and yeast in a stand mixer fitted with the dough hook. Add the eggs, milk and vanilla. Mix on medium-low speed for 5-7 minutes until smooth and elastic. With the mixer running, add the soft butter a spoonful at a time, letting it work in before adding more. Knead for 8-10 minutes until glossy and very stretchy. Scrape into a buttered bowl, cover and prove for 1½-2 hours at room temperature, until doubled in size.

2 Knock back the dough gently, then cover and chill for at least 1 hour (or overnight) to firm up, which makes shaping easier. Butter a 22cm (8½-inch) springform tin and line the base with baking parchment. On a lightly floured work surface, shape the chilled dough into a smooth ball, then flatten into a disc to fit the tin. Place inside, cover loosely and leave to prove for 45-60 minutes, until puffed and nearly doubled.

3 Preheat the oven to 180°C fan (400°F), Gas Mark 6. Brush the brioche gently with milk and sprinkle with pearl sugar or flaked almonds. Bake for 20-25 minutes until risen and deep golden. Cool in the tin for 10 minutes, then remove to a wire rack and leave until cold.

4 For the syrup, put the sugar and 60ml (4 tablespoons) of water into a small saucepan and heat gently, stirring, until the sugar dissolves. Simmer for 2 minutes, then remove from the heat and stir in the vanilla or orange blossom water. Leave to cool.

5 For the filling, heat the milk with the vanilla in a small saucepan until just steaming. In a

bowl, whisk the egg yolks, sugar and cornflour until smooth and paler. Slowly pour the hot milk over the yolk mixture, whisking constantly, then return to the pan. Cook over a medium heat, whisking, until thickened and just bubbling. Pour into a shallow dish, press clingfilm directly on to the surface to prevent a skin from forming and chill until cold.

6 When ready to fill the Tropézienne, whip the double cream with the icing sugar to soft peaks. Whisk the chilled custard to loosen, then gently fold in the whipped cream to make a light, spreadable cream.

7 Slice the cooled brioche horizontally in half with a long serrated knife. Brush the cut sides generously with the vanilla or orange blossom syrup. Spoon or pipe the cream over the bottom half in an even layer. Dot the raspberries evenly over the cream, nestling them in so they sit snugly.

8 Carefully set the top half of the brioche back on, pressing very lightly. Chill for at least 1 hour to set, then dust with icing sugar before serving.

LEMONY PISTACHIO ROULADE

SERVES 8

Far more impressive to serve than the effort it takes to make, this is fantastic for a celebration. A light pistachio-studded meringue – crisp outside and soft within – is rolled around clouds of whipped cream rippled with homemade lemon curd, but you can buy a good-quality pot if that's easier. It's a real showstopper, happily easy to roll and slice.

For the meringue

A little flavourless oil, for the tin
5 egg whites
280g (10oz) caster sugar
80g (2¾oz) pistachios, very finely chopped
Icing sugar, to dust

For the lemon curd and filling

150g (5½oz) unsalted butter, softened
280g (10oz) caster sugar
5 egg yolks
Finely grated zest and juice of 4 lemons
350ml (12fl oz) double cream, softly whipped

1 Preheat the oven to 180°C fan (400°F), Gas Mark 6. Line a 33 × 23cm (13 × 9-inch) Swiss roll tin with baking parchment and lightly oil the paper.

2 In a large, clean bowl, whisk the egg whites with an electric mixer on high speed until very stiff. Gradually add the sugar, a spoonful at a time, whisking until thick, stiff and glossy.

3 Spread evenly into the prepared tin and sprinkle the pistachios over. Bake for 10 minutes until lightly golden. Reduce the oven temperature to 140°C fan (325°F), Gas Mark 3 and bake for 15 minutes, or until the meringue feels firm. Remove from the oven, invert on to a sheet of baking parchment and carefully peel away the lining parchment. Leave to cool.

4 For the lemon curd, put the butter and sugar into a heatproof bowl and whisk by hand until combined. Stir in the egg yolks, then add the lemon zest and juice and whisk until smooth. Set the bowl over a pan of just-simmering water (the base of the bowl should not touch the water). Cook gently, whisking often, for 8–10 minutes, or until the curd has thickened enough to coat the back of a spoon. Do not let the water boil, or the curd may split.

5 Weigh out 100g (3½oz) of the lemon curd and set aside to cool. Spoon the rest into a sterilized jar (see page 17), seal and label. It will keep in the refrigerator for 2 weeks.

6 To fill the roulade, gently fold the reserved lemon curd through the softly whipped cream to create a marbled effect. Dust the meringue lightly with icing sugar, then spread the lemon cream over. Using a sharp knife, lightly score a line along a long side, about 1cm (½ inch) in from the edge. Using the paper to help you, roll up the meringue tightly from the scored edge. Transfer to a plate, seam on the bottom, and serve.

EASY RHUBARB TART

SERVES 8

My ode to the first forced rhubarb of the year, those slender pink stalks that arrive just when we're craving something bright and pretty. I spread a sheet of crisp puff pastry with a soft layer of vanilla cream, lining up rhubarb batons on top, still holding their shape but juicy and tender. A little rhubarb syrup and orange zest, and you have the most elegant, simple dessert.

1 ready-rolled all-butter puff pastry sheet
Ice cream or whipped mascarpone, to serve

For the crème anglaise
250ml (9fl oz) whole milk
150ml (¼ pint) double cream
1 vanilla pod, split and seeds scraped out
70g (2½oz) caster sugar
4 large egg yolks
1 tablespoon cornflour

For the rhubarb topping
400-500g (14oz-1lb 2oz) rhubarb, trimmed
80-100g (2¾-3½oz) caster sugar (depending how tart your rhubarb is)
Finely grated zest of ½ orange (optional but lovely), to decorate

1. Preheat the oven to 180°C fan (400°F), Gas Mark 6. Line a baking tray with baking parchment. Unfurl the puff pastry sheet on the tray and lightly score a 2cm (¾-inch) border. Gently press a fork along the border to create ridges. Bake for 15-18 minutes until puffed and golden. If the centre has risen, gently press it down with the back of a spoon.
2. For the crème anglaise, in a saucepan, heat the milk, cream, vanilla pod and seeds and half the sugar over a medium heat to just below a simmer, stirring to dissolve the sugar.
3. In a bowl, whisk the egg yolks, remaining sugar and cornflour until smooth and slightly pale. Pour the hot cream and milk mixture over the yolks, whisking, until light, fluffy and well combined. Pour back into the saucepan and return to a medium heat, stirring, until it just thickens to a light custard that coats the back of a spoon, but is still pourable.
4. Next, measure a rhubarb stalk across the pastry widthways and cut to fit, cutting all the rest to get a uniform look. (I use the cut-offs to make a compote.) Toss with the sugar in a shallow baking dish and roast in the oven for 10 minutes until just tender but still holding their shape. Leave to cool in the juices; reserve the syrup for glazing.
5. Pour a thin, even layer of the warm custard into the pastry. Arrange the rhubarb on top in rows, leaving a little custard visible, if possible. Bake for 15-20 minutes until the custard is just set with a slight wobble in the centre. The pastry should be deeply golden.
6. Carefully brush with the rhubarb syrup, to glaze the top, scatter with the orange zest, if using, and serve with ice cream or whipped mascarpone.

SUMMER RASPBERRY TRIFLE

SERVES 6–8

There is something wonderfully inviting about a big, generously layered trifle brought to the table, especially in summer when raspberries are at their peak. This version celebrates them in all their glory, folded into a jewel-like jelly that runs through every spoonful. The deep crimson colour alone makes it feel like a proper centrepiece before anyone has even dipped in. You can of course swap out the raspberries for strawberries, blackberries or mixed berries. If you happen to grow scented geraniums, their softly citrusy leaves lend a delicate, almost floral brightness to the berries as they infuse. If not, a few sprigs of lemon balm, verbena or mint will give a similarly fresh lift. Layered with tender Madeira sponge, silky mascarpone custard and a cloud of cream, this is a trifle that feels both nostalgic and quietly celebratory: perfect for a long, relaxed summer gathering... You will need a big trifle bowl, about 2.6 litres (4½ pints) in volume.

For the trifle layers

300g (10½oz) shop-bought or homemade Madeira cake, cut into 2.5cm (1-inch) pieces

500g (1lb 2oz) mascarpone

1 tablespoon vanilla extract

600ml (20fl oz) good-quality ready-made custard

400ml (14fl oz) double cream, softly whipped

A little shaved dark chocolate, to serve

For the raspberry jelly

8 gelatine leaves

1kg (2lb 4oz) raspberries, plus more to serve

100g (3½oz) caster sugar

6-8 scented geranium leaves, such as rose or lemon (optional, but lovely), or lemon balm, lemon verbena or mint

1. Scatter the cake pieces evenly in a large trifle bowl; mine is about 2.6 litres (4½ pints) in volume.
2. In a bowl, whisk together the mascarpone and vanilla until smooth. Gradually whisk in the custard until thick, silky and just pourable. Spoon it over the cake, spreading gently to the edges.
3. For the jelly, soak the gelatine leaves in a bowl of cold water for 5-10 minutes, until softened. Meanwhile, place the berries, sugar and geranium or other leaves, if using, in a large saucepan. Gently warm over a medium heat for 3-4 minutes, until the fruit softens and releases its juices. Remove from the heat. Lift out the geranium leaves and discard.
4. Squeeze the excess water from the softened gelatine and stir it into the warm raspberry mixture until fully dissolved. Set aside for 15-20 minutes, until no longer hot but still fluid.
5. Carefully ladle the raspberry mixture over the custard layer. Chill for 2 hours, or until softly set.
6. To finish, top with softly whipped cream, a scattering of raspberries and a little shaved dark chocolate just before serving. When serving, use a large and long spoon to scoop right down through all the layers, so every portion gets cake, fruit, jelly, mascarpone custard and cream.

Autumn & Winter

FRENCH ONION SOUP with garlicky Gruyère croutons

SERVES 4

Harry's favourite, and I love that this also happens to be (quietly) sort-of healthy. The onions are slowly cooked until sweet and caramelized, then deglazed with a little dry white wine before being simmered in good beef bone broth, so you're really eating a bowl full of onions, garlic and real stock rather than anything heavy or creamy. To make a simple broth, roast beef bones with an onion and carrot until browned, then simmer with water, herbs and a spoonful of tomato purée for several hours. The result is a rich, deeply flavoured base for those bubbling garlic, Gruyère and thyme croutons on top.

100g (3½oz) unsalted butter
8 onions, halved and thinly sliced
2 teaspoons clear honey
2 garlic cloves, finely grated or crushed
1 teaspoon dried oregano, or thyme leaves, or chopped rosemary leaves
100ml (3½fl oz) dry white wine
900ml (1½ pints) good-quality beef stock
Sea salt flakes and freshly ground black pepper

For the croutons

4 slices of sourdough bread
2 tablespoons olive oil, or melted unsalted butter
1 garlic clove, finely grated or crushed
1 teaspoon thyme leaves, or ½ teaspoon dried thyme
70g (2½oz) Gruyère, grated, plus more (optional) to serve

1. Place a heavy-based large saucepan over a medium heat and add the butter. Once it has melted, reduce the heat to low and stir in the onions. Cover and cook for 10 minutes, until soft.
2. Next, uncover the pan, stir in the honey and garlic and let the onions brown and slightly caramelize, stirring every few minutes until they become a deep golden colour. Stir in the dried or fresh herbs and season with salt and pepper.
3. Pour in the white wine and let it bubble for a minute or so to cook off the alcohol and dissolve all the sticky browned bits from the base of the pan, then pour in the stock and allow to cook for a further 30 minutes. Taste and adjust the seasoning.
4. To make the Gruyère croutons, preheat the oven to 180°C fan (400°F), Gas Mark 6. Cut or tear the bread into bite-sized cubes and place on a baking tray. In a small bowl, mix the olive oil or melted butter with the garlic, thyme, a pinch of salt and some pepper. Drizzle over the bread and toss to coat. Bake for 8–10 minutes, until the croutons are golden and crisp. Remove the tray from the oven, sprinkle the grated Gruyère over the hot croutons and return to the oven for 2–3 minutes, just until the cheese melts and clings to the bread.
5. Ladle the hot soup into warmed bowls and scatter generously with garlicky croutons and more cheese, if you like. Serve any extra croutons on the side, for topping up the bowls as you eat.

AUTUMN GRAIN SALAD

SERVES 4

One of my favourite ways to serve squash. The roasted squash and onions bring sweetness and caramelized edges, which sit beautifully against the chew of spelt or barley, toasted nuts and sharp bites of dried fruit. It's a generous bowlful that works as a main course with crusty bread, or a colourful side dish on a chilly evening, perhaps with Pumpkin Ravioli with Brown Butter & Sage (see overleaf), grilled sausages or roast chicken.

1 small butternut squash (about 600g / 1lb 5oz prepared weight), cut into 2cm (¾-inch) cubes
2 red onions, cut into wedges
2 tablespoons olive oil, plus more for the greens
1 teaspoon ground cumin
1 teaspoon clear honey, or maple syrup
200g (7oz) mixed grains, such as wholegrain spelt, pearl barley or coarse bulgur wheat
500ml (18fl oz) vegetable stock (for homemade, see page 125), or water
100g (3½oz) cavolo nero or Swiss chard, coarse stems removed, leaves finely shredded
60g (2¼oz) dried cranberries, or chopped dried apricots
60g (2¼oz) toasted nuts, such as walnuts, hazelnuts or pecans, roughly chopped
Handful of flat leaf parsley leaves
Small handful of mint leaves
60g (2¼oz) feta, or goat's cheese (optional)
Sea salt flakes and freshly ground black pepper

For the dressing

4 tablespoons extra virgin olive oil, plus more to serve
2 tablespoons red wine vinegar, or apple cider vinegar
1 teaspoon Dijon mustard
1 small garlic clove, finely grated or crushed
1 teaspoon clear honey (optional)

1 Preheat the oven to 200°C fan (425°F), Gas Mark 7. Tip the squash and red onions on to a large baking tray, drizzle with the oil, cumin and honey or syrup and season with salt and pepper. Toss well and roast for 25–30 minutes, turning once, until tender and caramelized at the edges. Leave to cool slightly.

2 Meanwhile, cook the grains in the stock or salted water according to the packet instructions, until just tender but still with bite. Drain well. Return them to the pan and add the greens with a drizzle of olive oil and a pinch of salt. Cover and let the residual heat gently wilt the leaves for 3–4 minutes, stirring once, until tender but still bright.

3 Whisk all the dressing ingredients together in a jug or bowl, seasoning to taste with salt, pepper and the honey, if you'd like more sweetness.

4 In a large bowl, combine the warm grains and greens with the roast pumpkin and onions, dried fruit, nuts and most of the herbs. Pour over the dressing and toss gently.

5 Transfer to a platter. Scatter over the remaining herbs and crumble the feta or goat's cheese on top, if using. Finish with a drizzle of extra virgin olive oil and a twist of pepper.

WINTER GREENS
with anchovy & garlic

SERVES 4 AS A SIDE DISH

There is nothing I love more in the depths of winter than a pan of dark, glossy greens, tangled with garlic and anchovy and shimmering with good olive oil. The anchovies melt away in the heat, leaving behind a deep, savoury backbone that makes humble cabbage or kale taste like something you'd find in a little trattoria on a cold night. This dish is wonderful with simply roasted meats – think roast chicken, pork or lamb – or with a steak (my favourite) or lamb chops. The greens are also beautiful alongside a creamy gratin or a roast fish (see pages 205 and 100), or spooned over thickly sliced sourdough toast with a poached egg on top for a very easy, supremely satisfying, healthy supper.

600g (1lb 5oz) mixed winter greens, such as cavolo nero, curly kale, Savoy cabbage or chard, coarse stems removed
3 tablespoons extra virgin olive oil, plus more to serve
4 anchovy fillets in oil, drained and chopped
3 garlic cloves, thinly sliced
Small pinch of chilli flakes (optional)
Juice of ½ lemon, or to taste
Sea salt flakes and freshly ground black pepper

1 Bring a large pan of salted water to the boil. Roughly shred the winter greens. Blanch the greens in the boiling water for 2–3 minutes until just tender but still bright, then drain well and lightly squeeze out any excess water.

2 In a large, wide frying pan, warm the olive oil over a medium heat. Add the anchovy fillets and stir for 1–2 minutes until they melt into the oil.

3 Add the sliced garlic and chilli flakes, if using, and cook gently for another minute until the garlic is fragrant but not browned.

4 Tip in the blanched greens and toss well in the anchovy and garlic oil. Fry for 3–4 minutes, turning often, until the greens are glossy, hot and starting to catch in little golden spots at the edges.

5 Squeeze over the lemon juice, season with a little salt and plenty of pepper (remember the anchovies are salty) and toss again. Taste and adjust with a touch more lemon juice or olive oil if you like. Serve straight from the pan in a warmed shallow bowl, with an extra drizzle of olive oil on top.

PUMPKIN RAVIOLI with brown butter & sage

SERVES 4 / MAKES ABOUT 36 RAVIOLI

In autumn, our Delica pumpkins climb and curl over the arches of the Walled Garden, hanging like lanterns above the beds. Their flesh is dense, sweet and brilliant orange: perfect for tucking inside silky sheets of homemade pasta. The nutty, aromatic butter catches on the ridges of the pasta and mingles with the sweet filling. A gentle, golden bowlful that tastes of the season.

For the filling

600g (1lb 5oz) Delica pumpkin, or other firm-fleshed squash, peeled and deseeded

2 tablespoons olive oil

40g (1½oz) finely grated Parmesan, plus more to serve

2 tablespoons mascarpone or ricotta

1 small garlic clove, finely grated or crushed

Leaves from a few thyme sprigs, or a pinch of dried thyme

Grating of nutmeg

Sea salt flakes and freshly ground black pepper

For the pasta

400g (14oz) Fresh Homemade Pasta (see page 126)

Semolina, or pasta flour, to dust

For the brown butter & sage

100g (3½oz) unsalted butter

Small handful (16–20) sage leaves

Squeeze of lemon juice

1 Preheat the oven to 200°C fan (425°F), Gas Mark 7. Cut the pumpkin into 3cm (1¼-inch) chunks and toss with the oil, salt and pepper. Spread on a baking tray and roast for 25–30 minutes, turning once, until very tender and lightly caramelized at the edges. Cool slightly.

2 Mash the warm pumpkin in a bowl or blitz briefly in a food processor until smooth but not completely puréed. Stir in the Parmesan, mascarpone or ricotta, garlic, thyme, a small grating of nutmeg and salt and pepper. It should be thick and scoopable. Leave to cool completely.

3 Roll the pasta dough into 1–1.5mm (1⁄16-inch) thick sheets (see page 126). On a lightly floured or semolina-dusted work surface, lay out 1 sheet and place heaped teaspoons or small mounds of pumpkin filling along it, spacing them well apart. Brush lightly around the filling with water. Lay a second sheet of pasta over the top, gently pressing out any air around each mound. Use a ravioli cutter, knife or pastry wheel to cut into individual raviolos, sealing the edges firmly. Dust with flour or semolina and set on a tray while you finish the rest.

4 Bring a large pan of well-salted water to a gentle boil. In a wide frying pan, melt the butter over a medium heat until it foams, then add the sage. Cook, swirling the pan, until the butter is a deep golden brown and the sage is crisp. Take off the heat and add a squeeze of lemon juice.

5 Drop the ravioli into the water and cook for 3–4 minutes, until they bob to the surface. Lift out with a slotted spoon, letting excess water drain off. Transfer to the warm butter, spooning it over. Divide between plates, spoon over the butter and finish with Parmesan and pepper.

CAPUTO

ROAST PORK
with apples & blackberries

SERVES 6

In early autumn, Harry heads off for hours every weekend to pick kilos of blackberries; he absolutely loves it, and I do too as I get a huge basket of berries to play with! Serve this with Rainbow Root Vegetable Gratin (see page 79), to soak up all the lovely apple and blackberry juices.

For the stuffing

60g (2¼oz) smoked pancetta, finely chopped
1 large shallot, finely chopped
200g (7oz) cooking apples, peeled, cored and chopped
30 blackberries
40g (1½oz) hazelnuts, lightly toasted and chopped
40g (1½oz) breadcrumbs
1 tablespoon finely chopped rosemary leaves
50g (1¾oz) butter, melted
Sea salt flakes and freshly ground black pepper

For the pork

1.5kg (3lb 5oz) boneless loin of pork
3 rosemary sprigs

For the sauce

400g (14oz) cooking apples, peeled, cored and chopped
20 blackberries
2 tablespoons caster sugar
50g (1¾oz) unsalted butter
1 rosemary sprig

1 Preheat the oven to 220°C fan (475°F), Gas Mark 9. Place a frying pan over a medium heat, add the pancetta and cook for 3–4 minutes until it turns golden. Scoop into a large bowl, leaving the fat in the pan. Add the shallot and cook gently for 3–4 minutes, until softened but not coloured. Tip into the bowl with the pancetta and leave to cool. Add the fruit, nuts, breadcrumbs, rosemary and melted butter, season generously, then mix well.

2 Butterfly the pork by making a lengthways slit along the middle, cutting just deep enough so it can be opened out flat (do not cut all the way through). Spoon the stuffing evenly over the cut side. Fold the loin back over and tie with kitchen string at even intervals so it returns to more or less its original shape, tucking in any stuffing that escapes.

3 Rub the pork all over with salt and pepper, then place in a roasting tray and tuck the rosemary sprigs around it. Roast for 25 minutes, then reduce the oven temperature to 160°C fan (350°F), Gas Mark 4 and cook for a further 20 minutes per 450g (1lb), or until the pork is cooked through and the juices run clear.

4 Meanwhile, make the sauce. Put all the ingredients into a saucepan with 100ml (3½fl oz) of water. Cover and cook gently for 15–20 minutes, stirring occasionally, until the apples have broken down. Once the pork is cooked, skim off about 100ml (3½fl oz) of its cooking juices and stir into the sauce. Remove the rosemary sprig and adjust the seasoning.

5 Transfer the pork to a board, cover loosely with foil and rest for at least 20 minutes. Carve thickly and serve with a big bowl of the warm apple and blackberry sauce.

A Hard-Working Kitchen

Designing a kitchen is a deeply personal process. The kitchen should be the heart of the home, drawing people in and holding them there, filled with warmth the moment they walk in. It is not just about how a space looks, but how it feels to live, cook and gather within it every day: a kitchen should support the rhythm of your life.

At Broadspear, I wanted a space that felt calm, generous and connected both to the landscape and to the way I cook and entertain. Every decision, from the smallest drawer to the overall flow of the room, was made with that in mind. Ultimately, when everything has its place, the kitchen becomes intuitive to use.

I started with function. It had been a tiny galley, so every decision needed to work hard to make it feel effortless to live in. I considered how I'd use the space: how I cook, where I prepare food and what I need within arm's reach. Every cupboard, drawer and work surface is planned so the kitchen supports me rather than slows me down.

Storage plays a huge role. I assigned a purpose to every drawer and cupboard before finalizing a design. Beside the oven, for example, I created slim drawers: one side for utensils, baking paper and clingfilm; the other for spices and dry ingredients. These small, thoughtful decisions make cooking feel seamless. At the centre, I designed a move-able island on wheels, with storage on both sides. Flexibility is key in a smaller kitchen and this allows me room to adapt.

Next, I turn to layout. In a small space, flow is everything, how you move through the kitchen and how to avoid restriction. I always create a working zone between fridge, oven, sink and dishwasher, all close to where I prepare food so I can move between them effortlessly. Otherwise, you waste so much energy moving back and forth. That sense of flow is essential. When it is right, cooking feels calm and intuitive. When it is not, even the most beautiful kitchen can feel frustrating to use.

Continuous counter space was a priority. My work surfaces run fluidly around the kitchen, giving plenty of room for preparation and cooking. Open shelving was key; by running shelves right to the ceiling, the eye is drawn upwards, creating a sense of height and allowing me to add personality through the pieces I display. The kitchen flows directly into the dining area, as I wanted it to feel like a continuous, connected space. A long table runs through the room, anchoring it and creating a natural place for gathering, eating and lingering.

Along the sides, I designed cabinets with glass doors to display glassware, ceramics and serving pieces. To enhance the sense of space, I painted the inside backs of the cabinets the same colour as the walls; this subtle detail allows the eye to move easily across the room, making it feel larger.

Lighting is hugely important; it is never just about visibility, it is about overall atmosphere. I approach lighting in layers. First, natural light: windows bring in brightness and connect the space to the outdoors. Then comes practical 'task lighting': focused light over work surfaces, the cooker and preparation areas. Finally, there is ambient lighting, which transforms the space. Soft lighting within cabinets, gentle wall lights and subtle illumination on shelves add depth as well as warmth. The softly lit wine shelves become a focal point as the day draws in, adding a layer of atmosphere. When these layers come together, the kitchen shifts beautifully from a functional workspace during the day to a warm, welcoming space at night.

Texture brings richness and character. Without it, even the most well-designed space feels flat.

I balance different materials to create contrast and interest. Glass-fronted cabinets feel light and open, while the lower cupboards are detailed with chicken wire to add a rustic edge. The white tiles, running from the work surface up to the first shelf, reflect light softly and bring a sense of freshness. Colour also plays an important role in texture. A gentle, fresh green – like a young sage leaf – has natural softness and depth, shifting beautifully with the light throughout the day. Hanging copper pots add a subtle gleam, while ceramics and glassware on open shelves add layers that feel personal and lived-in.

Warmth brings everything together, turning a kitchen into a space you want to spend time in. I chose a soft, cohesive palette of ivory tiles and colour-drenched walls, including that gentle green, to create a sense of continuity throughout the space. The colours all sit quietly together, feeling calm, expansive and comfortable. Underfoot, I chose stone paving that feels timeless. It stays cool in summer, while underfloor heating ensures it is warm and comforting in winter.

It is a kitchen designed not just for effortless cooking, but for gathering, sharing and living.

RAINBOW ROOT VEGETABLE GRATIN

SERVES 6

My way of celebrating the Walled Garden in all its autumn and winter glory. I slice whatever heritage roots are at their best – striped and golden beetroot, purple and orange carrots, parsnips, potatoes and celeriac – and layer them in colourful rows with thyme, garlic and cream. As the gratin bakes, the vegetables become tender, the top catches and caramelizes and the whole dish settles into something deeply comforting, but still bright and pretty on the table. Delicious served alongside my Roast Pork with Apples & Blackberries (see page 73), as the perfect cold-weather Sunday lunch.

2 tablespoons olive oil, or melted unsalted butter, for the dish
800g (1lb 12oz) mixed root vegetables, such as potatoes, carrots, parsnips, beetroot or celeriac, peeled
1 red onion, peeled
300ml (½ pint) double cream
150ml (¼ pint) whole milk
2 garlic cloves, finely grated or crushed
2 tablespoons thyme leaves, or 1 teaspoon dried thyme
60g (2¼oz) finely grated Gruyère, Comté or Parmesan, plus more for the top
1 tablespoon Dijon mustard (optional, but lovely)
Sea salt flakes and freshly ground black pepper

1. Preheat the oven to 180°C fan (400°F), Gas Mark 6. Oil or butter a baking dish (about 30 × 20cm / 12 × 8 inches).
2. Using a mandoline or a sharp knife, slice the mixed root vegetables and the red onion into thin rounds, 2–3mm (1/8-inch) thick. Keep the different colours in separate piles if you'd like to arrange them in rows or a spiral.
3. In a jug or bowl, whisk together the cream, milk, garlic, thyme, grated cheese and Dijon mustard, if using. Season generously with salt and pepper.
4. Arrange the sliced root vegetables in the dish, either in neat rows by colour for a rainbow effect, or in overlapping layers, tucking in slices of red onion evenly as you go. Try to keep the layers quite snug, so they cook evenly.
5. Pour the cream mixture evenly over the vegetables, tilting the dish gently so it settles between the layers. Sprinkle a little more cheese over the top.
6. Cover the dish loosely with foil or leftover butter wrappers and bake for 40 minutes. Remove the foil and bake for a further 25–30 minutes, or until the vegetables are tender to the tip of a knife and the top is bubbling and golden with some crispy edges. Allow to rest for at least 10 minutes before serving, so it settles and is easier to slice.

POACHED PEARS IN MARSALA with amaretti crunch

SERVES 4

We have four pear trees in the garden, each a birthday present from Harry, which feels like the loveliest kind of gift. They give us an abundant harvest, and this is my favourite way to show them off. The fruit turns jewel-like as it simmers gently in Marsala, citrus and spice. They look so chic for a winter dinner party, but are wonderfully simple to make ahead – keep the pears in their syrup, the mascarpone in the refrigerator and the crunch in an airtight container – then assemble just before your guests sit down.

For the pears

4 firm-but-ripe pears
150g (5½oz) caster sugar
300ml (½ pint) Marsala
Finely grated zest and juice of 1 orange
Finely grated zest of 1 lemon, plus 1 tablespoon lemon juice
1 cinnamon stick
2 star anise
4 cloves (optional)

For the amaretti crunch topping

60g (2¼oz) amaretti biscuits
20g (¾oz) flaked almonds
1 tablespoon demerara sugar
20g (¾oz) unsalted butter, melted

For the orange mascarpone

250g (9oz) mascarpone
100ml (3½fl oz) double cream
2 tablespoons icing sugar, sifted, or to taste
Finely grated zest of 1 orange, plus 1–2 tablespoons orange juice

1 Peel the pears, keeping the stalks intact, and slice a tiny piece off the bases so they can stand up. If you like, use a small knife or melon baller to remove the core from the base.

2 Put the sugar, Marsala, 300ml (½ pint) of water, the orange zest and juice, lemon zest and juice and spices into a wide saucepan that will hold the pears snugly in a single layer. Set over a gentle heat and stir until the sugar dissolves, then bring up to a simmer.

3 Lower the pears into the warm syrup, laying them on their sides if needed, and cover with a circle of baking parchment to help keep them submerged. Simmer very gently for 20–30 minutes, turning every now and then, until the pears are tender when pierced with the tip of a knife and a deep golden colour from the Marsala.

4 Once the pears are cooked, lift them out carefully with a slotted spoon and set aside on a plate. Increase the heat under the pan and bubble the poaching liquid for 8–10 minutes until it has reduced to a glossy, syrupy sauce that lightly coats the back of a spoon. Remove from the heat and leave to cool a little. Strain to remove the spices, if you want.

5 Meanwhile, make the topping. Preheat the oven to 160°C fan (350°F), Gas Mark 4. Crush

the amaretti into small, chunky crumbs and mix in a bowl with the almonds, demerara and melted butter. Spread on a small baking tray and bake for 6–8 minutes, stirring once, until golden and crisp. Leave to cool completely: it will firm up as it cools.

6 For the orange mascarpone, whisk the mascarpone, cream, icing sugar and orange zest together in a bowl until smooth and softly holding its shape. Add just enough orange juice to loosen it to a spoonable, billowy consistency. Taste and adjust the sweetness if needed. Chill until ready to eat.

7 To serve, spoon a generous dollop of mascarpone into the centre of each plate and use the back of the spoon to form it into a little nest. Stand a warm or room-temperature pear in the middle, then drizzle over some Marsala syrup. Scatter the amaretti crunch over and around, so you get soft fruit, cool cream and sweet, nutty shards in every spoonful.

THE PRETTIEST BLACKBERRY PIE

SERVES 6

There is something so charming about a blackberry pie, especially one with a woven lemon-scented lattice top and dusted with sugar so it bakes to a golden, sparkling crust. The simple filling lets the berries stay bright and juicy, just barely held together with sugar and spice. I love to bring it to the table slightly warm, with a jug of cream or a scoop of vanilla ice cream, and let everyone crack through the crisp pastry and dig down into the inky purple juices. Earlier in the year, you can use raspberries, strawberries, gooseberries or blackcurrants.

For the pastry

225g (8oz) unsalted butter, softened
55g (2oz) caster sugar
2 eggs
Finely grated zest of 1 lemon
340g (11¾oz) plain flour, plus more to dust

For the filling

300g (10½oz) blackberries
140g (5oz) caster sugar, plus more to sprinkle
1 teaspoon ground cinnamon
Finely grated zest of 1 lemon
1 egg, lightly beaten

1. To make the pastry, cream the butter and sugar together until pale and light. Beat in the eggs, one at a time, until combined. Add the lemon zest, then gently mix in the flour until the dough just comes together. Turn out on to a lightly floured board, bring it into a disc, wrap in clingfilm and chill for at least 1 hour; this helps it bake to a short, crumbly texture.
2. Cut off about two-thirds and roll it out on a lightly floured work surface to 3mm (about ⅛-inch) thick. Use it to line a 23cm (9-inch) pie plate or shallow dish, pressing it gently into the edges. Trim off excess pastry, then place in the refrigerator to chill for 20 minutes.
3. Spread the blackberries evenly over the pastry. Sprinkle with the sugar, cinnamon and lemon zest so the berries are lightly but evenly coated.
4. Roll out the remaining pastry on a lightly floured work surface to about 3mm (⅛ inch) thick and cut it into 10 even strips. Lay half across the pie in one direction, then weave the remaining strips over and under to create a lattice. Trim any overhanging pastry and crimp the edges all the way around to seal and neaten. Brush the lattice and edges with the beaten egg, then sprinkle generously with sugar. Chill again for about 30 minutes to firm up the pastry and help it hold its shape in the oven.
5. Preheat the oven to 180°C fan (400°F), Gas Mark 6. Bake the pie for 45-60 minutes, until the pastry is deep golden and crisp and the blackberry juices are bubbling up through the lattice. Transfer to a wire rack and leave to cool slightly. Serve warm or at room temperature, with softly whipped cream, a jug of pouring cream or good vanilla ice cream.

APPLE, CINNAMON & RAISIN BRIOCHE PUDDING

SERVES 6

If I had to eat just one pudding for the rest of my life, this would be it. The soft, buttery brioche soaks up the custard, the edges turn golden and crisp while the apples collapse into pockets of sweetness and the raisins become jammy and plump. I love to add a quick caramel sauce: melt 100g (3½oz) caster sugar in a saucepan until it turns a deep amber, then whisk in 50g (1¾oz) unsalted butter and 200ml (7fl oz) double cream with a pinch of sea salt flakes, and pour it, warm and glossy, over the pudding at the table: heaven!

80–100g (2¾–3½oz) unsalted butter, very soft, plus more for the dish
400ml (14fl oz) whole milk
400ml (14fl oz) single cream
120g (4¼oz) caster sugar
6 eggs
1 teaspoon vanilla extract
1 tablespoon ground cinnamon
1 large brioche loaf (500–550g / 1lb 2oz–1lb 4oz), sliced, then cut into triangles
250g (9oz) cooking apples, peeled, cored and thinly sliced
100g (3½oz) golden raisins
1–2 tablespoons demerara sugar (optional)

1 Preheat the oven to 160°C fan (350°F), Gas Mark 4. Lightly butter a medium-large ovenproof dish (about 2 litres / 3½ pints in volume).

2 Put the milk, single cream and 80g (2¾oz) of the caster sugar into a saucepan and warm gently over a medium heat, stirring, until the sugar has dissolved and the mixture is steaming but not boiling. Take off the heat and leave to cool until just warm.

3 In a large bowl, whisk the eggs with the remaining 40g (1½oz) sugar, the vanilla and cinnamon. Slowly whisk the warm milk mixture into the eggs to make a smooth custard.

4 Generously butter the brioche slices. Arrange one-third of them in the prepared dish, slightly overlapping, tucking in half the apples and raisins as you go. Repeat with another one-third of the brioche, then the remaining apples and raisins, and finally add a prettily arranged layer of brioche on top. Slowly pour the custard all over, giving it time to seep down into the layers. Use your hands or the back of a spoon to gently press the brioche into the custard so everything is well soaked. Leave to sit for 20–30 minutes so the brioche can absorb the custard.

5 Just before baking, sprinkle the top with demerara sugar, if using, for extra crunch. Bake for 40–45 minutes until the custard is just set in the middle and the top is puffed and deep golden, with crisp, caramelized edges. Leave to rest for 5–10 minutes.

6 Serve warm, with a jug of simple caramel sauce on the side (see recipe introduction), or a drizzle of cold cream, pouring it over so it runs into the little golden valleys of the pudding.

SMEG
9:34
SMEG

One-Pan Dinners

SPRING GREEN RISOTTO

SERVES 4

Spring at our farm in a single bowl, and one of the most beautiful dishes I make when the wild garlic appears in our woods and the first peas are ready in the garden. The vibrant green colour is utterly joyful on the plate, and the flavour is fresh, delicate and wonderfully seasonal. Blending some of the greens into a purée gives the rice a gorgeous emerald hue, while stirring through whole peas and wild garlic at the end adds texture and a lovely peppery bite. It's comfort food that tastes like springtime: creamy, bright and deeply satisfying.

1.2–1.5 litres (2–2½ pints) vegetable stock (for homemade, see page 125), or chicken stock
100g (3½oz) baby spinach
50g (1¾oz) wild garlic leaves, roughly chopped, plus more (optional) to serve
150g (5½oz) fresh or frozen peas
60g (2¼oz) unsalted butter, plus 50g (1¾oz) to serve
1 onion, finely chopped
2 garlic cloves, finely grated or crushed
300g (10½oz) arborio or carnaroli rice
150ml (¼ pint) white wine
75g (2¾oz) Parmesan, finely grated, plus more to serve
Finely grated zest and juice of ½ lemon
Sea salt and freshly ground black pepper

1 Bring the stock to a gentle simmer in a saucepan and keep it warm over a low heat.

2 Meanwhile, make a green purée: blanch the spinach in boiling salted water for 30 seconds, then plunge into ice-cold water. Drain well and squeeze out excess water. Blend the spinach, the wild garlic, half the peas and 200ml (7fl oz) of the warm stock until very smooth and bright green. Set aside.

3 Heat the 60g (2¼oz) butter in a large, wide pan over a medium heat. Add the onion and cook gently for 5–6 minutes until soft and translucent. Stir in the garlic and cook for 1 minute.

4 Add the rice and stir to coat in the butter, cooking for 1–2 minutes. Pour in the wine and stir until absorbed.

5 Now add the remaining warm stock a ladleful at a time, stirring frequently and allowing each addition to be absorbed before adding the next. This should take 18–20 minutes. The risotto should be gently simmering as you stir.

6 After about 15 minutes, when the rice is nearly cooked but still has a slight bite, stir in the green purée and the remaining whole peas. Cook for another 3–4 minutes until the rice is tender and creamy.

7 Remove from the heat and stir in the 50g (1¾oz) butter, the Parmesan, lemon zest and juice. Season to taste with salt and pepper, then cover and let rest for 2 minutes. Serve immediately, scattered with a few fresh wild garlic leaves if you like, more Parmesan and a twist of pepper.

WALLED GARDEN SOUP

SERVES 6

A true taste of our Walled Garden at Broadspear. It starts with a comforting base of root vegetables – carrots, parsnips and celery – gently cooked with rosemary and garlic until sweet and fragrant. I then add kale and cannellini beans for heartiness and texture, though chickpeas or butter beans work just as well. I love making this in huge batches out in my Pickling Shed, surrounded by crates of vegetables from the garden, then ladling it into cartons for the freezer. It's simple, nourishing and deeply connected to the seasons here at the farm.

3 tablespoons olive oil
3 carrots, finely chopped
3 parsnips, finely chopped
2 celery sticks, finely chopped
1 onion, finely chopped
2 teaspoons finely chopped rosemary leaves
3 garlic cloves, finely grated or crushed
1 litre (1¾ pints) chicken stock, or vegetable stock (for homemade, see page 125)
250g (9oz) cavolo nero, coarse stems removed, chopped or shredded
2 × 400g (14oz) cans of cannellini beans, drained and rinsed
Sea salt and freshly ground black pepper

To serve

50g Parmesan
1 tablespoon finely chopped rosemary leaves (optional)

1 Place a large saucepan or flameproof casserole over a low heat and pour in the olive oil, then stir in the carrots, parsnips, celery, onion, rosemary and garlic. Season with salt and pepper, stir well, cover and allow to cook for 15 minutes, stirring every 5 minutes or so.

2 Pour in the stock, stir and bring to the boil. Allow to cook for 10–15 minutes or until all the vegetables are cooked. Transfer to a food processor and blend until smooth, then return to the saucepan, or you can also blend this with a stick blender.

3 Add the cavolo nero and cannellini beans and cook for 3–4 minutes. Taste for seasoning.

4 Divide the soup between warmed bowls, grate over the Parmesan, sprinkle with rosemary if you like and serve.

ITALIAN MINESTRONE

SERVES 4

This recipe takes me straight back to my time living in Turin, where I first fell in love with this humble, nourishing soup. It was a weekly staple then, made with whatever vegetables were in season and affordable. Now, I make it even more special by filling it with freshly picked vegetables from our garden: carrots, courgettes, green beans and leafy greens, all at their sweetest and most tender. The combination of pasta and creamy cannellini beans makes it deeply satisfying, while the dried oregano and tomatoes bring that unmistakable Italian warmth. It's simple, wholesome and endlessly comforting.

2 tablespoons olive oil
1 onion, finely chopped
2 carrots, finely chopped
2 celery sticks, finely chopped
3 garlic cloves, finely chopped
1 tablespoon tomato purée
1 teaspoon dried oregano
400g (14oz) can of chopped tomatoes
1 litre (1¾ pints) vegetable stock (for home-made, see page 125), or chicken stock
1 bay leaf, torn
1 courgette, finely chopped
100g (3½oz) green beans, trimmed and cut into short lengths
400g (14oz) can of cannellini beans, drained and rinsed
100g (3½oz) small pasta (ditalini, small shells, or broken spaghetti)
2 handfuls of spinach, chard or cavolo nero, coarse stems removed, leaves chopped
Sea salt and freshly ground black pepper
Finely grated Parmesan, to serve

1 Heat the olive oil in a large, heavy-based pot over a medium heat. Add the onion, carrots and celery and cook gently for 8–10 minutes until softened. Stir in the garlic, tomato purée and dried oregano and cook for another minute until fragrant.

2 Add the chopped tomatoes, stock and bay leaf. Season with salt and pepper, bring to the boil, then reduce the heat to a gentle simmer. Cover and cook for 20 minutes.

3 Now add the courgette, green beans and cannellini beans. Simmer for another 10 minutes until the vegetables are tender.

4 Stir in the pasta and cook for 8–10 minutes, or according to the packet instructions, until it is just al dente.

5 Add the greens and cook for a final 2–3 minutes until wilted. Remove the bay leaf. Taste and adjust the seasoning.

6 Ladle into warmed bowls and serve with a generous grating of Parmesan, and crusty bread.

CREAMY GRUYÈRE & HAM BAKED EGGS

SERVES 2

One of my favourite fireside suppers, best enjoyed curled up with a glass of wine. It's gooey, soothing and surprisingly quick to make, yet feels wonderfully indulgent. The Gruyère melts into a rich, silky blanket around the eggs, while the crumbled ham adds salty, savoury depth. I love how versatile this recipe is too: you can swap in pancetta and Parmesan, or try tomatoes and olives, artichokes with Parmesan and parsley, crumbled black pudding, or even smoked salmon with chives. But this version, with nutty Gruyère and tender ham, is the one I come back to time and again.

25g (1oz) salted butter
60g (2¼oz) Gruyère, grated
1 teaspoon Dijon mustard
¼ teaspoon freshly grated nutmeg
½ teaspoon chopped thyme leaves
200ml (7fl oz) double cream
4 large eggs
80g (2¾oz) cooked ham, torn
Sea salt and freshly ground black pepper
Toast soldiers, to serve

1. Preheat the oven to 180°C fan (400°F), Gas Mark 6. Butter a 20cm (8-inch) ovenproof skillet or ovenproof dish with all the butter.
2. Place the cheese in a bowl and whisk together with the mustard, nutmeg, thyme and cream, with a pinch each of salt and pepper.
3. Spoon half the creamy cheese mixture into the prepared skillet or dish and crack the eggs on top. Spoon the remaining cheese mixture on top and sprinkle over the ham, or vice versa, depending whether you want crispy ham or not.
4. Place the skillet or dish on a baking tray and bake for 15 minutes. Serve with toasted bread cut into soldiers, so you can dip them into the eggs.

ZESTY LEMON LINGUINE ALFREDO

SERVES 4

An effortless ten-minute pasta, a one-pan, zest-brightened twist on a classic alfredo, finished with crunchy pine nuts. I still can't quite believe we manage to grow our own Amalfi lemons in the glasshouse; they're so sweet, fragrant and full of sunshine that I find ways to use them in everything. Here, there are just a few ingredients: lemon, butter, cream, Parmesan and a whisper of nutmeg. The lemon slices gently simmer in the sauce, infusing it with their bright, citrusy warmth, before the silky linguine is tossed through. Utterly delicious; a dream of Amalfi in a bowl. This is also good for a late-night supper.

500ml (18fl oz) double cream
1 lemon, finely zested, then thinly sliced
1 garlic clove, peeled but left whole
110g (4oz) salted butter, cut into small pieces
Grating of nutmeg
75g (2¾oz) Parmesan, finely grated, plus more to serve
500g (1lb 2oz) fresh linguine (for homemade, see page 126)
40g (1½oz) toasted pine nuts
1 tablespoon finely chopped flat leaf parsley leaves
Sea salt and freshly ground black pepper

1. Place a deep frying pan or saucepan over a medium-low heat. Pour in the cream and add the lemon zest and slices and whole garlic clove. Bring to a gentle simmer.
2. Next, gently whisk in the butter until melted. Remove and discard the garlic. Stir in the nutmeg and grated Parmesan, stirring until smooth, then season with salt and pepper.
3. Add the fresh linguine to the pan, making sure it sits in the sauce. Pour in about 100ml (3½fl oz) of hot water, then simmer gently, turning the pasta with tongs as it softens, for 4–5 minutes, or until the pasta is just al dente and the sauce has thickened and become glossy. Add a splash more hot water if the sauce becomes too thick before the pasta is cooked to your liking.
4. Remove and discard the lemon slices if you prefer a softer lemon flavour, or leave them there if you like. Taste and adjust the seasoning.
5. Scatter over the toasted pine nuts, more Parmesan and the parsley, then bring the pan straight to the table and serve.

HARRY'S AMAZING SCRAMBLED EGGS

SERVES 2

Pure weekend joy in our house. Once a week, Harry takes over the kitchen and somehow makes the best scrambled eggs I've ever tasted. Even after twenty-six years as a chef, I still can't replicate them. I'm convinced it's the alchemy of plenty of butter and his constant, patient stirring… oh, and of course the freshest eggs from our hens, but there's also just something special about being cooked for. The eggs turn out impossibly soft, creamy and silky every time, and they've become one of my absolute favourite things to eat, especially when I'm off duty and he's at the stove. I badgered him to write down exactly how he makes them, and here it is!

7 large eggs
50g (1¾oz) salted butter
Sea salt and freshly ground black pepper

1. Crack the eggs into a bowl and season with salt and a good twist of pepper. Whisk well to combine.
2. Melt the butter in a small saucepan over a medium-low heat.
3. Pour in the beaten eggs and stir continuously, making sure that the pan doesn't get too hot. You want the eggs to be creamy and smooth. Season to taste and serve on hot buttered toast.

ROASTED SEA BASS with sweet potatoes, spinach & caper salsa

SERVES 4

One of my favourite suppers when I pop by my lovely fishmonger Rex on my way home from work in London, wanting something light, fresh and a little bit special. The vibrant, zingy salsa cuts through the rich sweet potatoes beautifully and is absolutely gorgeous with the delicate, crispy-skinned fish. It looks impressive but comes together in under 40 minutes; perfect for when you want to eat well without hours spent in the kitchen.

4 sweet potatoes, peeled and cut into 2cm (¾-inch) cubes
3 tablespoons olive oil, plus more for the fish
2 whole sea bass (about 300g / 10½oz each), or 4 skin-on fillets, about 150g (5½oz) each
350g (7oz) baby spinach
Sea salt and freshly ground black pepper
Lemon wedges, to serve

For the salsa
Large handful of flat leaf parsley leaves, chopped
3 tablespoons capers, drained and chopped
1 garlic clove, finely chopped
Finely grated zest of 1 lemon and juice of ½ lemon
4 tablespoons extra virgin olive oil
Pinch of chilli flakes (optional)

1 Preheat the oven to 180°C fan (400°F), Gas Mark 6. Toss the sweet potato cubes with 2 tablespoons of the oil, salt and pepper on a large roasting tray. Spread out in a single layer and roast for 10 minutes if using whole fish or 20 minutes if using fillets, turning once.

2 Meanwhile, make the salsa: combine all the ingredients in a bowl, season and set aside.

3 For whole fish, pat dry with kitchen paper, score each side 2–3 times, rub inside and out with oil and season well, including in the cavity. Place on top of the sweet potatoes after those have roasted for 10 minutes, and drizzle with the remaining 1 tablespoon oil. Roast for 18–22 minutes, depending on size, until the flesh flakes easily from the bone.

4 For sea bass fillets, pat dry with kitchen paper and score the skin of each 2–3 times. Season both sides well with salt and pepper. After the sweet potatoes have roasted for 20 minutes, place the fillets on top, skin-side up, drizzle with the 1 tablespoon of oil and cook for 10–12 minutes, until just cooked through.

5 While the fish finishes cooking, wilt the spinach: place it in a colander and pour over a kettle of boiling water, or wilt it quickly in a saucepan with a splash of water. Drain well and season, then mix into the roasting tray with the sweet potatoes and fish.

6 Spoon the salsa generously over the fish and serve from the dish with lemon wedges.

SALMON, BROCCOLI & NOODLES

SERVES 2

My kind of fast food: fresh, vibrant and on the table in just ten minutes. Everything happens in one deep frying pan, which keeps both the washing-up and the fuss to a minimum. The salmon turns tender and flaky, the broccoli stays bright and just-cooked and the noodles soak up all the delicious cooking juices and sauce, topped with crunchy sesame seeds. It's the sort of dish I make on busy weeknights when I still want something nourishing and satisfying, but don't have the headspace for a long recipe: simple, wholesome and full of flavour.

1 tablespoon olive oil, plus more if needed
1 garlic clove, finely sliced
1 teaspoon chilli flakes
1 small head of broccoli, cut into small florets (total weight 200–250g / 7–9oz)
150g (5½oz) dried medium egg noodles
2 skinless salmon fillets (total weight about 250g / 9oz), cut into bite-sized pieces
1 tablespoon light soy sauce, plus more if needed
1 teaspoon toasted sesame oil
1 teaspoon clear honey
Sea salt and freshly ground black pepper

To serve (optional)
1 tablespoon toasted sesame seeds
Handful of mixed herb leaves

1. Place a shallow saucepan or a deep frying pan over a medium-high heat and add the olive oil. Add the garlic and chilli flakes, cook for about 30 seconds, then tip in the broccoli, noodles and 400ml (14fl oz) of water. Cover with a lid and simmer for 5 minutes, turning the noodles once or twice, until they are almost cooked.
2. Next add the salmon, with a pinch each of salt and pepper. Cover the pan and cook for 3–4 minutes, until the fish is just cooked through and flakes easily.
3. In a bowl, mix the soy sauce, sesame oil and honey. Pour it over the noodles. Toss together gently, trying not to break up the salmon too much, until everything is glossy and coated.
4. Taste and add a little more soy sauce or olive oil if needed. Serve in warmed bowls with toasted sesame seeds and herbs sprinkled on top, if you like.

CHICKEN MILANESE with rocket & Parmesan salad

SERVES 4

One of those effortlessly chic Italian dishes that never fails to impress. The chicken gets pounded thin, then coated in golden, crispy breadcrumbs spiked with lemon and Parmesan. It's simple but utterly delicious. I love piling it high with peppery rocket, more shavings of Parmesan and a squeeze of lemon juice: the contrast of the warm, crunchy chicken with cool, bright salad is perfect. It feels like something you'd order at a trattoria, yet it's surprisingly quick to make at home and always gets rave reviews around our table.

For the chicken

4 skinless chicken breasts
100g (3½oz) plain flour
2 eggs, lightly beaten
150g (5½oz) dried breadcrumbs (panko works brilliantly here)
50g (1¾oz) Parmesan, finely grated
Finely grated zest of 1 lemon, plus lemon wedges to serve
4 tablespoons olive oil
Sea salt and freshly ground black pepper

For the salad

100g (3½oz) rocket leaves
50g (1¾oz) Parmesan, shaved with a vegetable peeler
2 tablespoons extra virgin olive oil
1 tablespoon lemon juice
Handful of cherry tomatoes, halved (optional)

1 Place each chicken breast between 2 sheets of clingfilm or baking parchment. Use a rolling pin or meat mallet to bash them until about 1cm (½ inch) thick and evenly flattened.

2 Set up 3 shallow bowls: the first with the flour seasoned with salt and pepper, the second with the eggs, and the third with the crumbs mixed with the Parmesan and lemon zest.

3 Pat the chicken breasts dry with kitchen paper, then coat each first in the flour, shaking off any excess. Dip into the beaten egg to cover, then press into the breadcrumb mixture, making sure both sides are well coated.

4 Heat the olive oil in a large frying pan over a medium-high heat. Fry the chicken breasts for 3–4 minutes on each side until golden, crisp and cooked through. You may need to do this in batches. Drain on a plate lined with kitchen paper and keep warm.

5 Meanwhile, toss the rocket leaves with the shaved Parmesan, extra virgin olive oil and lemon juice. Season with a little salt and pepper. Add the cherry tomatoes, if using.

6 Serve each chicken Milanese topped with a generous pile of the rocket and Parmesan salad and a lemon wedge on the side.

WHOLE CHICKEN, BEAN & ROOT VEG CASSEROLE

SERVES 4

A recipe born out of testing my much-loved sage green casserole pot (see opposite for a photo), which is by far the number one bestseller in my online store. The pot fits a whole chicken perfectly, and I get enormous pleasure out of putting everything in together – beans, stock, white wine, herbs, garlic, celery, carrots, parsnips and chicken – then letting it all bubble away as one. It looks beautiful on the table, smells incredible and the flavours soak into each other as they cook. Minimal washing-up, too: absolute heaven!

80g (2¾oz) unsalted butter
1 chicken
8 whole shallots, peeled
2 celery sticks, sliced
5 carrots, peeled and chopped into 7.5cm (3-inch) pieces
5 parsnips, peeled and chopped into 7.5cm (3-inch) pieces
1 garlic bulb, halved horizontally
1 tablespoon tomato purée
250ml (9fl oz) white wine
1 litre (1¾ pints) chicken stock
700g (1lb 9oz) canned or jarred butter beans, drained and rinsed
4 thyme sprigs
4 flat leaf parsley sprigs
Juice of 1 lemon
Sea salt and freshly ground black pepper

1 Preheat the oven to 180°C fan (400°F), Gas Mark 6.

2 Melt half the butter in a large flameproof casserole over a medium heat. Season the chicken and brown it on all sides, about 10 minutes in total. Remove the chicken and set aside. Next add the remaining butter to the pot, and, once melted, add the shallots, celery, carrots, parsnips and garlic and cook for 5 minutes until browned, tossing every few minutes.

3 Stir in the tomato purée, followed by the wine, stock and beans. Return the chicken to the pot, breast-side up, and snuggle it into the vegetables. Next, add the thyme, parsley and lemon juice: flavour bombs! Season with salt and pepper.

4 Cover, transfer to the oven and cook for 1½ hours. Remove from the oven, keeping the lid on, and allow to rest in the pan for 20 minutes before serving.

EASY FAST CHICKEN CURRY

SERVES 4

My answer to those nights when only a curry will do. From the moment you start chopping to the moment it's on a tray in your lap, this takes about thirty minutes, yet it still feels like a proper, satisfying feast. About once a month, I get an unmistakable curry craving and nothing else will quite hit the spot. I love serving this with warm naan, fluffy basmati rice, a bowl of plain yogurt and a few good chutneys from my Pickling Shed, spread out in the middle of the table for everyone to share.

1 tablespoon olive oil
1 onion, finely chopped
3 garlic cloves, finely grated or crushed
1 tablespoon peeled and grated root ginger
2 teaspoons ground cumin
2 teaspoons paprika
1 teaspoon garam masala
3 tablespoons tomato purée
200g (7oz) natural yogurt
400ml (14fl oz) hot chicken stock
Juice of 1 lemon
400g (14oz) cooked chicken, shredded (bought, leftovers or cooked specially)
Sea salt and freshly ground black pepper

To serve

2 microwave pouches of basmati rice
4 store-bought naan
250g (9oz) natural yogurt
Your favourite chutneys
Handful of herbs (optional)

1 Place a saucepan or flameproof casserole over a low heat and add the olive oil. Stir in the onion, garlic and ginger, cover and cook for 2 minutes. Next remove the lid and add the cumin, paprika, garam masala and tomato purée. Stir and cook for 2 minutes more.

2 Stir in the yogurt, hot stock and lemon juice, then season with salt and pepper.

3 Tip in the cooked shredded chicken and stir well, then cook for a final 10 minutes.

4 Meanwhile, warm the rice and naan according to the packet instructions. Serve the curry with the rice, naan, yogurt and chutneys, scattering over the herbs, if you like.

SPICY SAUSAGE PASTA

SERVES 6

A true crowd-pleaser, loved by all ages around the table. I suggest using chorizo here, but any good spicy sausage will work beautifully. We keep pigs in our woods and a few years ago I developed my own sausage, flavoured with chilli, fennel, oregano and garlic, and that's the one I love to use here. The sausages bubble away with black olives, tomato, rosemary, bay, a little more chilli and plenty of garlic to create a rich, deeply savoury sauce. It's a big, generous, one-pan dish bursting with exciting flavour.

1 tablespoon olive oil
400g (14oz) cooking chorizo, sliced into 2.5cm (1-inch) pieces
3 garlic cloves, finely grated or crushed
1 large red chilli, thinly sliced
2 × 400g (14oz) cans of plum tomatoes
100ml (3½fl oz) tomato passata
1 tablespoon finely chopped rosemary leaves
1 bay leaf
14 black olives, pitted and crushed
500g (1lb 2oz) dried casarecce pasta, or penne, fusilli or rigatoni
Sea salt and freshly ground black pepper

To serve (optional)
Finely grated Parmesan
Handful of basil leaves

1. Place a shallow flameproof casserole or large saucepan over a medium heat and add the olive oil. When the oil is hot, stir in the sliced chorizo and cook for 6–7 minutes, stirring every minute or so, until the sausage is browned.
2. Reduce the heat to low, stir in the garlic and chilli and cook for a minute. Next add the plum tomatoes, passata, rosemary, bay and olives and season with salt and pepper.
3. Now stir in the pasta, coating it with the liquid. Cover and allow to cook for 10 minutes, stirring every few minutes to make sure nothing is sticking at the bottom of the pan. If the sauce is getting dry, add a few tablespoons of water.
4. Once the pasta is cooked, serve in warmed bowls with Parmesan and basil leaves scattered over, if you like, and a big green salad on the side.

OUR HOUSE 'CHEFFIE' MUSHROOM & GRUYÈRE OMELETTE

SERVES 1

The omelette I make most often at home, using beautiful fresh eggs... we have twenty hens, so there are lots of eggs to use up at our farm! I love making it 'cheffie'-style: thin, delicate and folded into that classic restaurant oval. The nutty Gruyère melts into the earthy mushrooms and the whole thing feels indulgent, yet takes just minutes to make.

Knob of unsalted butter (about 15g / ½oz)
75g (2¾oz) chestnut or button mushrooms, thinly sliced
3 fresh eggs, ideally from your own hens!
40g (1½oz) Gruyère, grated
1 tablespoon chopped flat leaf parsley leaves, or chopped chives
Sea salt and freshly ground black pepper

1. Heat half the butter in a medium nonstick frying pan (about 20cm / 8 inches) over a medium-high heat. Add the mushrooms and cook for 3–4 minutes until golden and any liquid has evaporated. Season with salt and pepper, then transfer to a plate and keep warm. Wipe out the frying pan.
2. Lightly beat the eggs in a bowl with a pinch each of salt and pepper until just combined; don't overwork them.
3. Heat the remaining butter in the frying pan over a medium-high heat. When it's foaming, pour in the eggs. Tilt the pan and use a spatula to draw the edges towards the centre, letting the uncooked egg flow to the sides.
4. After about 30 seconds, when the omelette is nearly set but still slightly runny on top, scatter the cooked mushrooms and grated Gruyère down the centre.
5. Tilt the pan and use your spatula to carefully fold one-third of the omelette over the filling, then roll it over again to create a neat, restaurant-style oval shape. Let it cook for another 10–15 seconds.
6. Slide on to a warmed plate, seam-side down. Scatter with herbs and serve immediately.

SAUSAGE, FENNEL & APPLE TRAYBAKE

SERVES 4

Pure autumn comfort. The combination of sweet roasted apples, caramelized fennel and golden sausages is absolutely heavenly, and it all happens in a single tray with almost no effort. I love using apples from our orchard, which we planted eight years ago and now rewards us with the most delicious fruit every season. The apples soften and sweeten as they roast, their juices mingling with the honey and balsamic to create a gorgeous sticky glaze. It's hearty, warming and wonderfully satisfying, perfect for a relaxed family supper.

2 fennel bulbs, trimmed and cut into thick wedges
2 eating apples, such as Gala or Braeburn, cored and cut into wedges
1 large red onion, cut into wedges
500g (1lb 2oz) baby potatoes, halved
3 garlic cloves, whole and unpeeled
3 rosemary sprigs
4–5 thyme sprigs
3 tablespoons olive oil
2 tablespoons clear honey
2 tablespoons balsamic vinegar
8 good-quality pork sausages
Sea salt and freshly ground black pepper

1. Preheat the oven to 180°C fan (400°F), Gas Mark 6.
2. Place the fennel, apple and onion wedges, halved potatoes and garlic cloves in a large roasting tin, setting aside any fennel fronds for serving the dish later. Strip the leaves from the rosemary and thyme sprigs and scatter over the vegetables.
3. Drizzle over the olive oil, honey and balsamic vinegar. Season generously with salt and pepper, then toss everything together with your hands until well coated. Nestle the sausages into the vegetables, spacing them evenly. Prick each sausage a few times with a fork, so their juices can mingle with the vegetables.
4. Roast for 40–45 minutes, turning the sausages halfway, until they are golden and cooked through and the vegetables are tender and beginning to caramelize at the edges.
5. Toss the roasted vegetables gently to coat them in the pan juices. Transfer to a serving platter, top with the sausages and scatter over any reserved fennel fronds. Serve with crusty bread or creamy mashed potatoes, to soak up the lovely juices.

BEEF SHIN RAGU

SERVES 6

My idea of true comfort cooking. Shin is an underrated cut, full of flavour and natural gelatine, which melts down into the richest, silkiest sauce when given time and a gentle heat. I brown the meat well, then slow-cook it in robust red wine, good beef stock, tomatoes and cinnamon, which adds gentle sweetness and earthy warmth. After a couple of hours, the meat collapses into tender shreds and the sauce turns velvety and deep. I always make a big pot and freeze portions for those days when I have no time to cook at all.

500g (1lb 2oz) boneless beef shin
1–2 tablespoons olive oil
1 onion, finely chopped
1 carrot, finely chopped
1 celery stick, finely chopped
2 garlic cloves, finely grated or crushed
2 teaspoons thyme leaves
½ cinnamon stick
3 tablespoons tomato purée
200ml (7fl oz) red wine, ideally a type high in tannin, such as Chianti, Cabernet Sauvignon or Bordeaux
250ml (9fl oz) beef stock (for homemade, see page 64)
400g (14oz) can of plum tomatoes
Sea salt and freshly ground black pepper
Finely grated Parmesan, to serve

1. Preheat the oven to 160°C fan (350°F), Gas Mark 4 and season the beef all over with salt.
2. Set a flameproof casserole over a medium heat and add 1 tablespoon of olive oil. Once the oil has warmed, brown the meat very well on all sides, then remove and set aside.
3. Add another tablespoon of oil to the pan, if needed, and add the onion, carrot, celery, garlic, thyme, cinnamon and a little more salt. Cover and cook over a medium-low heat for 10–15 minutes until the vegetables are soft.
4. Stir in the tomato purée until everything is well coated and continue to cook for another few minutes. Then return the browned beef to the pan, pour in the red wine, stir well and leave for 10 minutes to cook.
5. Next, pour in the beef stock and tomatoes, using the back of a wooden spoon to crush the tomatoes. Season with salt and pepper, cover with a lid and bring the ragu up to a simmer.
6. Place in the oven for 2 hours.
7. Once the ragu is cooked, remove the cinnamon stick. Serve in warmed bowls with pasta, placing Parmesan on the table for everyone to help themselves.

GUINNESS BEEF STEW

SERVES 6

Pure winter solace for me. It starts with the most delicious beef from our Aberdeen Angus cattle on the farm, which becomes meltingly tender when slow-cooked in a rich, savoury sauce. I love making stews like this when the weather turns cold; it feels generous, deeply warming and full of homely nostalgia. Growing up in Ireland, a hearty beef casserole was a regular fixture at our table. And there is nothing else I would dream of serving with it than buttery creamy mashed potatoes or Buttery Colcannon (see page 197), piled high, to soak up every last bit of gravy!

50g (1¾oz) unsalted butter
Olive oil
150g (5½oz) bacon lardons, or pancetta
300g (10½oz) shallots, whole and peeled
6 carrots, cut into 5cm (2-inch) lengths
1kg (2lb 4oz) stewing beef, cubed
400g (14oz) chestnut mushrooms, quartered
1 litre (1¾ pints) stout, such as Guinness
1 bouquet garni, or 3 thyme sprigs
Sea salt and freshly ground black pepper

1. Preheat the oven to 160°C fan (350°F), Gas Mark 4.
2. Start by browning all the ingredients. Place a flameproof casserole over a medium heat and melt the butter with a splash of olive oil, then stir in the bacon, followed by the shallots and carrots. Cook until golden brown, then transfer to a plate.
3. Next add the beef to the pot with a little more oil if needed, season with salt and pepper and cook until browned all over. Transfer to the plate.
4. Place the mushrooms in the pot and cook for 2 minutes. Season to taste and transfer to the plate.
5. Pour the stout into the pot and use a whisk to scrape off all the bits stuck to the bottom of the pot (this is where the flavour is). Next, return all the browned ingredients, followed by the bouquet garni or thyme, then stir and cover.
6. Place the casserole in the oven for 2 hours. Serve with creamy mashed potato, or Buttery Colcannon (see page 197).

Weekend Staples

CLODAGH'S SODA

MAKES 1 LOAF

The loaf I grew up eating in Ireland, and to which I return every single Saturday morning. It's everything I love in a bread recipe: quick, simple and wonderfully forgiving. There's no kneading, no proving, no waiting around... just stir, shape and bake. The bread is tender and slightly crumbly, with a gorgeously crunchy, golden crust. I love adding rosemary for its fragrant contrast to the tangy yogurt in this recipe, but you can use thyme instead, or leave the herbs out entirely. You can also swap the milk and yogurt for 600ml (20fl oz) of buttermilk, depending on what you have.

200g (7oz) plain flour
2 teaspoons bicarbonate of soda
350g (12oz) wholemeal flour, plus more to dust
1 teaspoon sea salt flakes, plus more to sprinkle
2 tablespoons finely chopped rosemary leaves (optional)
350ml (12fl oz) whole milk
250g (9oz) natural yogurt

For the glaze
50ml (1¾fl oz) mix of milk and yogurt

1. Preheat your oven to 220°C fan (475°F), Gas Mark 9.
2. Sift the plain flour and bicarbonate of soda into a large bowl, then stir in the wholemeal flour and salt. Using clean hands, mix in half the rosemary, if using, then make a well in the centre.
3. Separately whisk together the milk and yogurt and slowly pour it into the well, using your free hand to mix the flour into the liquid; try and spread your fingers far apart while you do this. Make sure there are no dry patches and that the dough is completely wet.
4. Pat your hands with flour, shape the dough into a round and place it on a floured baking tray. Flour a large knife and cut a deep cross into the top of the dough, slicing about two-thirds of the way through.
5. Brush the loaf with the milk and yogurt mixture using a pastry brush; this will give a lovely golden colour to the bread once baked. Evenly sprinkle with the remaining finely chopped rosemary, if using, and some sea salt flakes.
6. Bake for 25 minutes, then reduce the oven temperature to 180°C fan (400°F), Gas Mark 6 and bake for a further 25 minutes. To test whether the loaf is cooked, tap the base with your knuckles; it should sound hollow. Leave to cool on a wire rack.

AÏOLI

MAKES 200G (7OZ)

On Saturday mornings at Broadspear, I whisk up a big bowl of aïoli and instantly feel like I've got half the weekend's cooking done. With our farm eggs – from hens that roam all over the fields – it turns impossibly rich and golden, and becomes the sauce I reach for with almost everything. I spoon it alongside grilled prawns or roast chicken, tuck it into sandwiches, set it out as a dip with crisp garden crudités, or fold it through new potatoes or crab for the easiest salad. Having a jar of this in the refrigerator always feels like having a meal ready and waiting.

2 egg yolks, at room temperature
1 teaspoon Dijon mustard
100ml (3½fl oz) extra virgin olive oil
100ml (3½fl oz) vegetable oil
Finely grated zest and juice of 1 lemon
1 garlic clove, finely grated or crushed
Sea salt and freshly ground black pepper

1. Crack the eggs yolks into a bowl, add the mustard, and lightly whisk by hand.
2. Measure out both oils into a jug. Using a hand whisk, slowly whisk the mixed oils in a very light drizzle into the egg yolks. The aïoli will gradually turn thick and creamy.
3. Stir in the lemon zest and juice and the garlic, then season with salt and pepper. Stored in the refrigerator, this will last for a week.

HARRY'S NOT-SO-SECRET SALAD DRESSING!

MAKES 300ML (½ PINT)

I call this 'not-so-secret' because everyone that tries it at our house asks Harry to show them how he makes it. It's become A Thing! It's the most delicious creamy, zingy and slightly sweet dressing that transforms a simple green salad into something wow! It lasts in the refrigerator for ages, about a month.

100ml (3½fl oz) apple cider vinegar
200ml (7fl oz) extra virgin olive oil
1 teaspoon Dijon mustard
1 teaspoon clear honey
Sea salt and freshly ground black pepper

1. Place all the ingredients in a bowl and whisk together, or pour them into a jam jar, seal and shake well.
2. Check the flavour and adjust the seasoning if necessary.

BROADSPEAR GARDEN VEGETABLE BROTH

MAKES 5 LITRES (8¾ PINTS)

At Broadspear, the contents of my vegetable garden are always the starting point for this broth. I love using all the trimmings that might otherwise be discarded: the feathery tips of asparagus, deep green leek leaves, French bean ends and whatever else the garden is giving. I avoid starchier vegetables such as potatoes, turnips and parsnips, which can make the broth cloudy, and instead layer in flavour with fresh or dried mushrooms and a whole garden of veg. Once I have a big pot of broth made, usually on a Saturday morning, it becomes the quiet backbone of my weekend cooking. It is a warming cup of nourishment on its own, or can be the start of a quick soup, a silky risotto, a pan gravy, or a simple supper with poached chicken.

6 carrots, chopped
2 onions, chopped
2 celery sticks, chopped
3 tomatoes, chopped
5 mushrooms, sliced
Small bunch of flat leaf parsley
6 black peppercorns
Sea salt

1. Put all the vegetables in a large flameproof casserole with the parsley and peppercorns and cover with 6 litres (10½ pints) of water.
2. Bring to the boil, then reduce the heat and allow to simmer uncovered for 2 hours. You want the liquid to reduce slightly, to concentrate the flavour.
3. Skim any foam off the top for a nice clear broth, then ladle it through a sieve into a large bowl. Press the vegetables in the sieve gently with the back of the ladle to extract more liquid and flavour. Taste and adjust the seasoning (don't add salt any earlier than this, as it would make it too strong once reduced).
4. Allow to cool, then refrigerate for up to 3 days, or freeze in portions.

FRESH HOMEMADE PASTA

MAKES 6 SERVINGS

There's a deep sense of nostalgia for me when I make fresh pasta. I first learned how to make it as a chef at Ireland's famous Ballymaloe House, and soon after, I began selling it at the Saturday morning farmers' market in Midleton, County Cork. On Friday nights, after finishing my shift at the restaurant, I'd return to my cottage and spend hours making kilos of pasta for the next day. I've always loved the magic of transforming simple flour and eggs into something so utterly spectacular. More than twenty years later, it's still a ritual I return to most weekends, now using beautiful fresh eggs from our hens. Served simply with salty butter, fragrant sage and a generous grating of Parmesan, it remains one of life's most satisfying and pure dishes.

500g (1lb 2oz) pasta flour
Large pinch of sea salt
4 egg yolks, plus 3 whole eggs
Olive oil, if needed
Semolina flour, to dust

1. Pile the flour into a mound on a clean wooden board, salt it generously, then make a wide well in the centre. Pour the yolks and whole eggs into the well, then beat the egg mixture with a fork, slowly pulling in the flour from the sides until it has all been absorbed. If the dough is still a bit dry, add olive oil to loosen.
2. Knead the dough by pressing the heel of one hand into the ball, keeping your fingers high, while pushing it firmly away from you. The dough should stretch and roll under your hand to create a shell-like shape. Turn the dough over, then press into it with your knuckles, one hand at a time. This process should be carried out around 10 times. Roll the dough back into a ball, wrap it in clingfilm and allow it to rest at room temperature for at least 20–30 minutes.
3. Lightly dust a work surface with semolina and shape the dough into a rectangle, then cut it into quarters. Wrap each piece you are not working on in clingfilm, to stop it from drying out. Set up a pasta machine and push the first one-quarter of dough through the rollers 8 times. With each pass through the rollers, reduce the setting, until you reach the final (thinnest) setting. Be careful your pasta does not break, as you should now have a long thin sheet.
4. Cut the long sheet in half and sprinkle both sides with semolina. Hang up one half of the sheet on a clean clothes horse (or something similar) to dry slightly for a few minutes. Set up the pasta machine with your selected cutters and run the other half of the pasta sheet though the machine to cut it into pappardelle (2–3cm / ¾–1-inch wide strips), tagliatelle (1cm / ½-inch wide strips), tagliolini (5mm / ¼-inch wide strips), or whichever type of pasta you wish. Hang the cut pasta on the clothes horse. Repeat with the other half sheet of pasta.
5. Repeat the process with the remaining three-quarters of the dough.
6. When it is all done, place the cut pasta on a board, sprinkle over semolina and gently toss through. Then use a fork to twirl it into little pasta 'nests' and place them on a baking sheet. Cover and chill until you are ready to use it. Store in the refrigerator and eat within 2 days.

EXTRA VIRGIN OLIVE OIL
EXTRA VIRGIN OLIVE OIL
WILDSMITH
WILDSMITH

ALL-PURPOSE ROASTED GARDEN TOMATO SAUCE

MAKES ABOUT 1 LITRE (1¾ PINTS)

My favourite way to deal with a glut of glasshouse tomatoes, though it works just as beautifully with good shop-bought ones. The result is a deeply savoury, silky sauce that seems to go with everything, from a quick bowl of pasta or a tray of roast chicken, to forming the base of a shakshuka, spooned over grilled fish or lamb, or spread on pizzas and flatbreads. You can keep it simple, or build in extra flavour with olives, basil leaves, anchovies or capers, or loosen it with a little stock or cream for a quick soup. Having a jar of this in the refrigerator over a lazy weekend always feels like a last-minute supper waiting to happen!

2kg (4lb 8oz) ripe tomatoes, halved or quartered
4 garlic cloves, thinly sliced
4 thyme sprigs
3–4 tablespoons extra virgin olive oil
Sea salt and freshly ground black pepper

1. Preheat the oven to 160°C fan (350°F), Gas Mark 4. Arrange the tomatoes in a single layer on a large roasting tray.
2. Scatter over the sliced garlic and thyme, drizzle with the olive oil and season generously with salt and pepper. Toss gently on the tray, then turn the tomatoes cut-sides up.
3. Roast for 30–40 minutes, or until the tomatoes are soft, caramelized at the edges and releasing their juices.
4. Tip everything from the tray – tomatoes, juices, garlic, thyme and oil – into a blender or food processor and blend until you have a silky-smooth sauce.
5. Taste and adjust the seasoning, then use straight away, or cool and store in the refrigerator for up to 3 days, or freeze in portions for easy future meals.

GARDEN GREEN JUICE

SERVES 2

At weekends, I walk out to the Walled Garden and pick greens to juice with just-pulled carrots, an apple from the orchard, celery, parsley and a little ginger. For ten years, I've started every day with vegetable juice and it has quietly transformed my life... from how I feel in my skin, to my energy levels, to the way I move through the day with more mindfulness.

2 big handfuls of spinach, chard or kale
3 carrots
1 apple
6 celery sticks
5cm (2-inch) piece of root ginger, peeled and sliced
2 flat leaf parsley sprigs

1 Just wash and dry all the ingredients and then pass them through a juicer.

2 Serve with a couple of ice cubes, if you like your juice chilled.

ROSEMARY & SEA SALT CRISPBREADS

MAKES 8

One of my favourite weekend staples: long, elegant shards of golden crisp dough that look beautiful on a table and seem to go with everything. I'll pile them up beside drinks with a bowl of dip, tuck them alongside starters or a main course, or sometimes scatter them straight down the centre of a tablescape. They're unbelievably simple to make. Once you've rolled them out, you can scatter over rosemary and sea salt as I do here, or ring the changes with chopped olives or sun-blushed tomatoes. They'll keep happily for up to three days in an airtight container.

½ teaspoon fast-action dried yeast
210g (7½oz) plain flour, plus more to dust
2 tablespoons olive oil, plus more for oiling and brushing
Leaves from 3 rosemary sprigs, finely chopped, plus more for sprinkling
Sea salt flakes

1. Pour 100ml (3½fl oz) of warm water into a bowl, sprinkle in the yeast and whisk together well. Leave for 5 minutes until the mixture starts to foam.
2. Sift the flour into a large bowl and make a well in the centre. Pour the yeast mixture into the well and add the olive oil and a sprinkle of salt. Stir together until a dough forms: it should be moist but not sticky.
3. Tip the dough on to a floured work surface and knead for 10 minutes. Transfer to an oiled bowl, cover with a clean tea towel or clingfilm and place in a warm, dry spot, such as an airing cupboard, for 1 hour.
4. Preheat the oven to 180°C fan (400°F), Gas Mark 6. Line a large baking sheet, or a couple of regular-sized baking sheets, with baking parchment. Divide the dough into 8 equal pieces and roll out each piece on a lightly floured work surface into a rectangle measuring about 24 × 10cm (9½ × 4 inches). Transfer to the prepared baking sheet(s). Brush with olive oil and sprinkle evenly with the chopped rosemary and sea salt flakes.
5. Bake for 15 minutes or until crisp and golden. (You may have to bake these in batches.) Remove from the oven and leave to cool on wire racks.

Our Animals

The animals at Broadspear are not just residents of our home: they are the quiet workforce that has helped to repair the soil and turn the land into a truly sustainable small farm. When we arrived, the fields and woods felt tired and compacted, their energy a little dulled by time and neglect. Over the years, our Aberdeen Angus cattle, woodland pigs, hens and Aylesbury ducks have stitched life back into the place, one hoof print, snuffle, peck and paddle at a time.

The Aberdeen Angus herd brought the first real sense of scale and presence to the fields. Watching them graze slowly across the pasture, heads down, moving as a calm, steady group, you begin to understand what proper, managed grazing can do for land. Their weight presses seeds into the soil, their hooves break up hard ground, and their dung feeds an entire unseen world of insects and microbes. Instead of fields being over-grazed or left to scrub, the cattle move through in a field rotation system, trimming back the grass, fertilizing as they go, then we give each area time to rest and recover. Year by year, the pasture has grown thicker and more diverse – we now have wild orchids, clover and beautiful grasses growing – and the soil underneath is so wonderfully rich. All thanks to our beautiful cattle.

In the woods, the pigs have been busy with their own particular kind of restoration. Just a few months after they made the five-acre woodland their home, they had cleared all the overgrown brambles and set about clearing, rooting and turning the ground as efficiently as any machine, but with far more care. Their strong snouts break up compacted earth, as well as work fallen leaves and twigs back into the ground, creating a rough mulch that holds moisture and feeds the soil. Places that were once impenetrable have become open, dappled spaces where new plants can take hold. The pigs live well – roaming, wallowing, sleeping under trees – and in return they leave behind a woodland floor that is renewed rather than depleted and exhausted.

Closer to the house and garden, the hens are constantly, quietly at work. They patrol the cutting beds and vegetable rows, picking off slugs and insects, scratching at the top layer of soil and dust-bathing wherever the sun lands. Each tiny scratch helps to aerate the surface; each dropping is a little packet of fertilizer. Over time, the ground they move across becomes looser, richer and more crumbly, perfect for growing. They turn kitchen scraps and garden trimmings into eggs and compost, closing loops that might otherwise leak away as waste. Their presence weaves animal life through the most productive parts of the farm, making the gardens feel less like set pieces and more like living ecosystems.

The Aylesbury ducks bring a different energy – softer, more fluid – but their impact on the land is just as real. They waddle through the orchards and along the edges of beds, delicately hoovering up slugs, snails and other pests that would happily devastate tender leaves. Unlike chickens, they are gentler on the soil surface, their webbed feet spreading their weight and leaving only the lightest impression. Around ponds and damp patches, they help keep ecosystems in balance, turning potential problems into protein, and their manure, like that of the other animals, ultimately returns to the soil as part of the farm's compost and fertility.

Duckies foraging, July 2024

Harry with our first piglets the day they arrived, September 2023

Very happy to be holding my first Burford Brown hen

Our piggies' first taste of Broadspear apples, September 2023

The girls making themselves at home, May 2021

With our Aberdeen Angus herd, June 2022

With the little pigs when they arrived, September 2023

Harry with his girls, August 2022

With the snowy ducks, April 2022

What all these animals share is a kind of partnership with the land. None of them are here by accident; each species has been chosen and managed to do the work it is naturally good at, in a way that benefits both animal and earth. The cattle cycle nutrients through the pasture, the pigs reset and enrich the woodland, the hens knit fertility through the gardens, while the ducks keep pests in check and water margins lively. Together, they have taken a piece of land that once felt tired and, season by season, turned it into a thriving, sustainable patchwork of fields, woods and gardens.

When I look across Broadspear now, I don't just see animals on land; I see land and animals shaping one another. The soil underfoot is darker and more resilient, the pastures more diverse, the woods more open and rich. Our small farm works because of this web of life: hooves, snouts and beaks all playing their parts. The animals give us delicious food, of course, but they also give us something more lasting: a living, breathing system that can carry Broadspear forward, year after year, in balance.

Canapés & Cocktails

MY FAVOURITE MARTINI!

MAKES 1

My kind of martini: cold, crisp and with just the right salty edge. It's my go-to, whether I'm easing into a dinner party or winding down at the end of the day. I like everything properly chilled, so I pop my glasses in the freezer for an hour or two before serving, and I always store my bottles of vodka in the freezer. I'm firmly a stirred-not-shaken girl, and I keep it to about twenty seconds so it stays silky and strong. I always save the brine from jars of olives just for this and serve it with three plump green olives on top. Classic, unfussy and absolutely perfect!

Ice cubes
75ml (2½fl oz) vodka
7.5ml (1½ teaspoons) dry vermouth
7.5ml (1½ teaspoons) olive brine
3 green olives on a cocktail stick, to serve

1. Fill your martini glass with ice while you mix the drink, to get it very chilled.
2. Fill a cocktail shaker with ice. Pour in the vodka, vermouth and olive brine. Stir for 25 seconds until very cold.
3. Discard the ice from the martini glass and strain the cocktail into the chilled glass. Serve with the green olives on a cocktail stick.

CACIO E PEPE CHEESE STRAWS

MAKES 12

A wonderfully simple nibble that always disappears far too quickly. Inspired by the classic Roman pasta dish, these bring together that irresistible combination of sharp cheese and plenty of black pepper, all wrapped up in crisp, golden puff pastry. I love serving them with drinks, whether at a casual gathering in the kitchen or something a little more celebratory, as they're the perfect companion to a chilled glass of something sparkling. It's lovely to place a big glass filled with these crunchy twists on the table for everyone to help themselves: they feel generous, relaxed and so moreish. They're also incredibly handy to have up your sleeve, as you can prepare them a few days ahead and keep them in the refrigerator, ready to pop into the oven before guests arrive.

You can easily swap the Parmesan for Cheddar or Gruyère, depending on what you have. The key is to be generous with both cheese and pepper, letting the bold flavours shine through.

1 ready-rolled all-butter puff pastry sheet
1 egg
Splash of milk
50g (1¾oz) Parmesan, finely grated
50g (1¾oz) pecorino, finely grated
Sea salt flakes and freshly ground black pepper

1. Line a baking tray with baking parchment. Unroll the sheet of puff pastry and set it, on the paper it comes in, on a work surface. Crack the egg into a cup and beat it with the milk with a fork. Brush both sides of the pastry sheet with the egg wash.
2. Evenly sprinkle three-quarters of the Parmesan and pecorino over the sheet of pastry, followed by a good few twists of freshly ground black pepper. Gently press the cheese and pepper into the pastry.
3. Using a sharp knife, cut the pastry into 12 even strips. Holding each end, twist each strip 3-4 times, then pinch the ends to help it keep its shape. Place the twists on the prepared tray, evenly spaced apart. Grate the remaining cheese over each straw and add a sprinkle of sea salt flakes.
4. Place the tray in the refrigerator for about 10 minutes. The chilling will help give a lovely crispness once baked. Preheat the oven to 180°C fan (400°F), Gas Mark 6.
5. Place the tray in the oven and bake for 18-20 minutes, until the straws are golden and crisp, then carefully transfer to a wire rack to cool and crisp up. Serve them in a glass, or laid out on a platter.

THE BLOODY HARRY

SERVES 1

This is firmly Harry's drink, and I can say with complete confidence that nobody, and nowhere, makes a Bloody Mary quite like he does. It's become something of a Sunday ritual in our house; at about midday, he'll make up a big batch to sip while poring over the papers and pottering away, getting lunch underway. Harry has a way of getting the balance so perfectly: a good kick of spice, plenty of citrus and that savoury depth that makes a Bloody Mary so satisfying. He always insists on using Clamato juice, and I have to agree, it really does make all the difference, giving extra savoury depth and richness. Served over ice with a crisp stick of celery, it's such a great pick-me-up!

1 shot of vodka
Juice of ½ lemon
3 dashes of Worcestershire sauce
3 dashes of Tabasco sauce
180ml (6fl oz) Clamato juice
Pinch of celery salt
Freshly ground black pepper

To serve
Ice cubes
½ celery stick

1. Pour the vodka, lemon juice, Worcestershire sauce, Tabasco sauce and Clamato juice into a glass, season with celery salt and freshly ground black pepper and mix well with a spoon.
2. Clatter ice cubes into a glass and pour in the Bloody Mary, add a celery stick and serve.

WHIPPED LEMON RICOTTA on focaccia squares

MAKES 12

These little bites are fresh, light and full of flavour, but with just the right touch of indulgence. The whipped ricotta is soft and creamy with the bright lift of lemon and basil, while a sprinkle of chilli flakes adds a gentle warmth that lingers beautifully.

I love serving this on focaccia, but toasted sourdough, crisp crostini or even good crackers work just as well. For something a little more special, I often finish them with a drizzle of honey or a slow-roasted tomato on each square, which adds a lovely sweetness and depth. They're simple to put together, but feel effortlessly elegant.

For the whipped lemon ricotta

250g (9oz) ricotta
Finely grated zest of 1 lemon
Small handful of basil leaves, finely chopped
1 tablespoon olive oil
Sea salt

To serve

Focaccia, cut into 12 small squares
Pinch of chilli flakes
Clear honey or slow-roasted tomatoes (optional, see page 129)
Basil leaves

1. Place the ricotta, lemon zest, basil, olive oil and a pinch of salt into a bowl. Using a whisk or a fork, whisk until smooth, light and creamy.
2. Spoon or pipe the whipped ricotta on to the focaccia squares. Finish with a light sprinkle of chilli flakes and, if you like, a drizzle of honey or a spoonful of slow-roasted tomatoes, or basil leaves. Serve immediately.

AUTUMN FORAGED BLACKBERRY, THYME & ORANGE COCKTAIL

SERVES 8

A cocktail just made for autumn evenings when wellies are kicked off at the door, the fire is just beginning to crackle and the kitchen is full of chatter... my kind of heaven! Inspired by hedgerow foraging and bowlfuls of blackberries gathered from around the hedgerows at Broadspear, it's a drink that feels both a little wild and wonderfully cosseting.

I love setting up a little 'help yourself' cocktail table and letting everyone dive in and make their own. A jug of majestic blackberry syrup, thyme sprigs scattered about, bowls of berries, curls of orange zest and a hand-written menu card to guide the way: it's relaxed and so fun. The drink is fresh, fragrant and gently sparkling, with just enough sweetness to feel like a proper autumn treat.

For the blackberry syrup

460g (1lb) blackberries, plus more to serve
200g (7oz) granulated sugar
2–3 thyme sprigs, plus more (optional) to serve
200ml (7fl oz) fresh orange juice, plus the finely grated zest from the oranges

For the cocktail

Ice cubes
Twists of orange zest
600ml (20fl oz) chilled vodka
Chilled soda water

1. Start by making the syrup. Place the blackberries, sugar and 500ml (18fl oz) of water in a saucepan over a medium heat and gently bring to the boil, stirring until the sugar is dissolved. Add the thyme, then remove from the heat and leave to cool and infuse. Once fully cold, stir in the orange juice and zest. Cover and chill until ready to serve.
2. When you are ready to serve, fill each glass halfway with ice and add a thyme sprig, if using, a blackberry and a twist of orange zest. Fill the glass one-quarter full with blackberry syrup and one-quarter with vodka, then top up with soda water.
3. Give each drink a gentle stir so the syrup, vodka and soda just combine. Serve immediately, while still cold and sparkling.

WALLED GARDEN ROASTED ROOT VEGETABLE CRISPS

MAKES 2–3 BOWLS

I love big bowls of these on the table; they're beautiful, colourful, simple to make and you can play endlessly with different vegetables and flavourings. I love that I can make something fun with root veg during autumn and winter. I make a tray or two ahead of time and keep them in an airtight jar, ready to bring out with drinks, alongside a dip, or scattered over salads and soups for extra crunch.

Choose 3-5 vegetables, about 800g (1lb 12oz) in total, for a mix of colours and flavours:
Beetroot (red, golden or candy-stripe)
Carrots (orange, purple or yellow)
Parsnips
Sweet potato
Celeriac
Turnips

For the seasoning
2-3 tablespoons olive oil
Sea salt flakes

Optional flavourings (choose 1-2 per batch):
Finely chopped rosemary or thyme leaves
Smoked paprika, or sweet paprika
Ground cumin, or ground coriander
Chilli flakes
Finely grated lemon zest, or orange zest

1. Preheat the oven to 150°C fan (340°F), Gas Mark 3½. Line 2 large baking trays with baking parchment. Scrub the veg and peel if needed. Using a mandoline or sharp knife, slice as thinly and evenly as possible: thinner slices will be crisper. Pat dry with kitchen paper.
2. In a large bowl, toss the vegetable slices with the oil, just enough to coat lightly. Add salt and any flavourings, and toss again so everything is evenly seasoned. Arrange in a single layer on the trays; they should overlap as little as possible so they roast rather than steam.
3. Roast for 20-35 minutes, depending on thickness and veg type, turning the trays and flipping thicker slices halfway through. They're ready when the edges are crisp and the centres dry. Keep an eye on them towards the end, as they can scorch quickly. Leave to cool completely on the trays; they will firm up further. Taste and add more salt if needed.

Storage

Once completely cool, store in an airtight tin, with a small piece of baking parchment inside to help absorb any moisture. They're best eaten within 2–3 days, when they're at their crispest and most fragrant; if they soften slightly, refresh them on a baking tray in a low oven for a few minutes.

THE CORK ARMS SMOKY

MAKES 2 (WITH A TOP UP FOR BOTH!)

The very first cocktail we ever made in our little pub in the woods, so it's a special drink for us. It is also the cocktail that Harry and I created together when we first started dating! There's something about it that feels instantly comforting: the warmth of the whiskey, the gentle smokiness and that soft citrus lift that makes it just right for cold evenings.

This is our go-to cocktail through the winter months, the kind you sip slowly by the fire with good company and muddy boots by the door. It's rich and warming, but the lemon and orange keep it bright, while the egg white gives it a beautiful, velvety top.

125ml (4fl oz) smoky whiskey
4 dashes of Angostura bitters
70ml (2½fl oz) simple sugar syrup (see below)
Juice of 1 lemon
juice of ½ orange, plus 2 orange slices
2 egg whites
Ice cubes

1 Place the whiskey, bitters, syrup, lemon and orange juice, egg whites and ice in a cocktail shaker. Shake for 2 minutes.
2 Pour into chilled coupe glasses and serve with the orange slices.

How to make a simple sugar syrup

If you're a fan of cocktails, this is extremely handy to keep in the refrigerator, where it will last in an airtight container for up to 3 months.

1 Place equal weights of white sugar and water in a saucepan, depending on how much syrup you want to make. Set over a medium heat.
2 Stir to dissolve the sugar. If it threatens to boil, reduce the heat. When the sugar has dissolved, it is ready. Leave to cool, then decant into an airtight container and refrigerate.

HONEY & ROSEMARY ROASTED NUTS

MAKES 500G (1LB 2OZ)

I love having these on hand, so I make a big batch, pour them into a large jar and keep them ready for impromptu grazing boards, or a little something to nibble with a cocktail or a glass of wine. They're gently sweet, lightly salted and perfumed with rosemary, which makes them feel a little more special than regular nuts. You can play with herbs and flavourings: thyme or sage work beautifully; a pinch of smoked paprika or chilli flakes adds warmth; orange zest and ground cumin takes them in a completely different direction.

2 tablespoons clear honey
1½ tablespoons olive oil, or melted unsalted butter
2 teaspoons finely chopped rosemary leaves
1 teaspoon sea salt flakes, plus more to taste
½ teaspoon freshly ground black pepper
¼ teaspoon chilli flakes, or a pinch of smoked paprika, for gentle heat (optional)
500g (1lb 2oz) mixed unsalted nuts, such as almonds, cashews, pecans and hazelnuts

1. Preheat the oven to 170°C fan (375°F), Gas Mark 5 and line a baking tray with baking parchment. In a large bowl, whisk together the honey, oil or melted butter, rosemary, salt, pepper and, if using, the chilli flakes or smoked paprika until you have a smooth, glossy mixture. Add the nuts and toss well so they're evenly coated.
2. Spread the nuts in a single layer on the prepared tray, making sure they're not piled on top of each other. Roast for 15 minutes, stirring once or twice, until the nuts are golden and smell toasty. Keep a close eye on them towards the end, as they can catch quickly.
3. Remove from the oven and leave to cool completely on the tray; the coating will firm up and turn lightly crisp as they cool. Taste and add a little more salt if needed. Once fully cooled, transfer to a large jar or airtight container. They keep well for up to 2 weeks.

AIR FRYER MINI CRAB CAKES

MAKES 18–20

Perfect when you want to offer something a bit more substantial to your guests, these feel generous and satisfying, while still being easy to serve and eat. They're wonderfully convenient too, as you can prepare and shape them the day before, then simply cook them off in the air fryer just before serving. If you prefer to use a conventional oven, bake them at 180°C fan (400°F), Gas Mark 6 for 12–15 minutes, turning halfway, until golden and heated through. I serve them warm, with a dollop of aïoli on top, which adds a lovely creamy richness.

400g (14oz) white crab meat
2 slices of stale white bread, whizzed into fine crumbs
2 dashes of Worcestershire sauce
½ tablespoon chopped dill, plus more fronds and flowers to serve
1 tablespoon aïoli (for homemade, see page 124), or good-quality mayonnaise, plus more to serve
Finely grated zest and juice of ½ lemon, plus more zest (optional) to serve
Olive oil
Sea salt and freshly ground black pepper

1. Place all the ingredients except the olive oil in a bowl, season well and mix gently until just combined. Shape into small, bite-sized patties, 4-5cm (2 inches) wide. You should get 18-20 of them. Place on a tray and chill in the refrigerator for at least 1 hour to firm up.
2. Preheat the air fryer to 180°C (400°F). Lightly brush or spray the crab cakes with olive oil and place them in a single layer in the air fryer basket (you may need to cook them in batches rather than crowd them too much).
3. Cook for 8-10 minutes, turning halfway through, until golden and heated through.
4. Serve warm, with a bowl of aïoli to dollop on top and a sprinkle of dill fronds or flowers and lemon zest, if you like.

BROADSPEAR HONEY, GORGONZOLA & DATE BITES

MAKES 16

One of my favourite things to serve over Christmas and the winter months, these are simple, indulgent and always one of the first things to disappear. They feel wonderfully festive without any effort, and are perfect for passing around with drinks or adding to a grazing table. I love how they bring that balance of sweet and savoury in one perfect mouthful: rich, moreish and just a little bit special.

16 dates
80g (2¾oz) Gorgonzola
1 tablespoon clear honey
30g (1oz) pistachios, finely chopped

1. Using a sharp knife, cut a slit lengthways in each date and remove the stone. With a teaspoon, spoon Gorgonzola cheese inside each date and place on a serving platter.
2. Drizzle the honey on top, followed by a generous sprinkle of the pistachios. That's it!

CHICORÉE
SSONNADE
IN MINUTES

Delicious Suppers

A BIG POT OF CREAMY PANCETTA & GARLIC MUSSELS

SERVES 2

Growing up in Ireland, big steaming pots of mussels were a regular sight on the table. My dad absolutely loved them, and there was something so soothing about everyone reaching into the same pot, shells clinking, mopping up the juices with thick slices of bread. This version is a little more indulgent, with smoky pancetta, garlic and a splash of white wine and cream to create the most delicious broth. The mussels stay tender and sweet and the smoked pancetta brings a gentle warmth and depth. Served with buttery sourdough to soak up every last drop, it feels like a very simple kind of feast for two, perfect for a Friday night at home.

1kg (2lb 4oz) mussels
30g (1oz) salted butter
2 shallots, finely chopped
100g (3½oz) smoked pancetta, chopped
3 garlic cloves, finely grated or crushed
100ml (3½fl oz) single cream
100ml (3½fl oz) white wine (ideally something lemony, such as Sauvignon Blanc)
2 tablespoons finely chopped flat leaf parsley leaves
Sea salt and freshly ground black pepper
Lemon wedges, to serve

1. Start by prepping the mussels. The shells should be tightly shut and, if not, should promptly close if you tap them with your finger. If they do not close, they are not alive and should be discarded. Many mussels will have a 'beard', which is a clump of fibres they use to navigate and attach themselves to rocks on the seabed, or to ropes. Before cooking, this beard will have to be removed. To do this, give the beard a sharp tug and pull it towards the hinge of the mussel before discarding. (Do this at the last minute.)
2. Next, rinse the mussels in cold water to remove any sand, and, using a knife, scrape off any barnacles. (You don't have to remove barnacles, but it is easy and makes the dish look neater.)
3. Melt the butter in a large saucepan over a medium-low heat. Stir in the shallots, cover and sweat for 2 minutes; you want them soft and translucent. Remove the lid, add the smoked pancetta and cook for 1 minute, then stir in the garlic and cook for a further minute.
4. Increase the heat to high and stir in the cream and white wine, followed by the mussels. Season with salt and pepper, stir well, cover and cook for 6–8 minutes, or until the shells are all open, gently shaking or stirring the pan now and then. Lastly, stir in the parsley.
5. Serve with lemon wedges for squeezing and slices of buttered sourdough or chunks of baguette to mop up the delicious juices.

FARM FRUIT SKILLET CRUMBLE

SERVES 4–6

Some of my favourite puddings are those that come out a little different every time you make them. On the farm, there's always something coming into season, and this simple skillet crumble has become a way of gathering whatever's at its best into one warm, golden pudding. One week it might be peaches and plums, another blackberries, pears and windfall apples, all bubbling away together under a nubbly, buttery topping. I love bringing the skillet straight to the table so everyone can scoop out big spoonfuls, still warm and fragrant, with cream, or custard, or ice cream melting over the top. It's the kind of everyday farmhouse dessert that is so easy to make and feels so warming and cosy. When there's only two of you sharing it, there's enough here for seconds, or to save for breakfast the next day.

For the fruit

800–900g (1lb 12oz–2lb) mixed ripe fruit, such as peaches, plums, apples, figs or blackberries
70g (2½oz) caster sugar
1–2 tablespoons cornflour (use 2 tablespoons if the fruit is very juicy)
1 teaspoon vanilla extract
Juice of ½ lemon

For the crumble

120g (4¼oz) plain flour
80g (2¾oz) rolled oats
80g (2¾oz) light brown sugar
½ teaspoon ground cinnamon (optional)
50g (1¾oz) almonds, hazelnuts or walnuts, chopped
100g (3½oz) cold unsalted butter, chopped

1 Preheat the oven to 160°C fan (350°F), Gas Mark 4.

2 Pit or core and slice peaches, plums or apples; slice figs; leave berries whole. In a bowl, toss the fruit with the caster sugar, cornflour, vanilla and lemon juice. Tip into a 24cm (9½-inch) ovenproof skillet or frying pan and spread out evenly.

3 For the topping, mix the flour, oats, brown sugar, cinnamon, if using, and nuts in a bowl. Add the cold butter and rub it in with your fingers until you have a rough, clumpy crumble.

4 Scatter the crumble evenly over the fruit, leaving a few small gaps so steam can escape.

5 Bake for 30–35 minutes, until the crumble is golden and the fruit is bubbling up around the edges. Let it sit for 10 minutes to settle, then serve warm from the skillet with cream, ice cream or custard.

HONEYED PEAR, RADICCHIO & GORGONZOLA SALAD

SERVES 4

Honeyed pears, bitter leaves and salty cheese are one of those timeless combinations that feel both elegant and effortless. I love this salad for cosy autumn or winter suppers, when pears are at their sweetest and you want something light but still special. The warm, honeyed pear slices are tucked into the radicchio leaves, with creamy Gorgonzola and a bright orange-scented dressing bringing everything together. A final scatter of pistachios adds crunch and colour, making this a beautiful little plate to start a meal. It's also fabulous scaled up for a dinner party, as you can get everything plated an hour beforehand and just add the dressing at the last minute.

For the salad

2 tablespoons clear honey
2 large ripe pears, quartered, cored and sliced
Large head of radicchio, leaves separated
160g (5¾oz) Gorgonzola
Finely grated zest of 2 oranges
80g (2¾oz) pistachios, roughly chopped

For the dressing

2 tablespoons balsamic vinegar
4 tablespoons olive oil
2 teaspoons clear honey
2 tablespoons fresh orange juice
Sea salt and freshly ground black pepper

1. Make the dressing in a small bowl or jug by whisking together the balsamic vinegar, olive oil, honey and orange juice. Season well to taste, then set aside.
2. Place a nonstick frying pan over a medium heat. Drizzle in the honey and, once it starts to bubble, add the sliced pears. Cook the slices for 2–3 minutes on each side until lightly caramelized and just tender, then remove from the heat.
3. Arrange the radicchio leaves on a serving plate. Nestle the warm honeyed pear slices among the leaves, then crumble over the Gorgonzola and scatter with the orange zest and pistachios.
4. Spoon the dressing over the salad just before serving, and finish with a little sprinkling more black pepper, if you like.

CREAMY ROASTED SQUASH, CARAMELIZED ONION & SAGE TART

SERVES 4

There's something about roasted squash, sweet onions and sage that always makes me think of slow, cosy afternoons in the kitchen. The oven does most of the work, softening the squash and turning the onions sticky, while you simply layer everything on to a sheet of pastry. I buy the puff pastry; make sure it's the all-butter variety, it makes such a difference. I add a blanket of creaminess underneath with ricotta or crème fraîche, which makes the tart feel extra comforting without any fuss. Baked until puffed and golden, it's the kind of easy lunch or supper you can bring straight to the table, slice, then share with a simple green salad and a glass of wine.

300g (10½oz) peeled and deseeded squash, cut into small cubes or slim crescents
2 tablespoons olive oil
1 tablespoon unsalted butter
2 onions, thinly sliced
1 ready-rolled all-butter puff pastry sheet
150g (5½oz) ricotta, or crème fraîche
1 teaspoon finely chopped sage leaves, plus more sage leaves to serve
100g (3½oz) grated hard cheese, such as Gruyère or mature Cheddar
Sea salt and freshly ground black pepper

1 Preheat the oven to 180°C fan (400°F), Gas Mark 6. Toss the squash with 1 tablespoon of the olive oil and a little salt and pepper and spread on a baking tray in a single layer. Roast for 20–25 minutes until golden and tender.

2 Meanwhile, warm the remaining 1 tablespoon olive oil and the butter in a frying pan over a low heat. Add the sliced onions with a pinch of salt and cook gently for 15–20 minutes, stirring now and then, until soft, golden and caramelized.

3 Unroll the puff pastry on to a baking tray lined with baking parchment (or use the paper the pastry comes wrapped in). Lightly score a 2cm (¾-inch) border around the edge with a knife, without cutting all the way through, and prick the centre with a fork.

4 In a small bowl, loosen the ricotta or crème fraîche with a fork and season with a little salt and pepper. Spread it evenly over the centre of the pastry, staying inside the scored border. Top with the caramelized onions and roasted squash. Sprinkle over the chopped sage and grated cheese, then season again lightly.

5 Bake for 20–25 minutes, until the pastry is puffed and golden and the cheese is melted and bubbling. Leave to cool for a few minutes, then scatter with sage leaves, slice and serve warm.

VANILLA PANNACOTTA with honeyed figs

SERVES 4

This always feels like the most elegant and palatable way to end a meal, while secretly being one of the simplest desserts to make. This version is all about that soft, gentle wobble: rich with cream, scented with real vanilla and just sweet enough. I love pairing it with warm honeyed figs, roasted with a little butter and rosemary until they're tender and syrupy. Spoon them over the chilled pannacotta and you get a beautiful contrast of cool and warm, creamy and fragrant, that feels effortlessly special, and it is also delicious with peaches, plums or pears cooked the same way. The extra winning thing about this is that you can make it the day before.

For the pannacotta

2 gelatine leaves
400ml (14fl oz) double cream
100ml (3½fl oz) whole milk
1 vanilla pod, split lengthways
40g (1½oz) caster sugar

For the figs

2 tablespoons unsalted butter, melted
2 tablespoons clear honey
Leaves from 1 rosemary sprig, finely chopped
4 ripe figs, quartered

1. For the pannacotta, place the gelatine leaves in a bowl of cold water and leave to soften for 5–10 minutes.
2. Meanwhile, pour the cream and milk into a saucepan. Add the vanilla pod and sugar, then set over a medium-low heat. Gently warm until just below the boil, stirring to dissolve the sugar, then reduce the heat and simmer very gently for 3–5 minutes to infuse. You do not want it to thicken or reduce too much.
3. Take the pan off the heat. Lift out the vanilla pod and scrape the seeds into the warm cream, whisking them in. Squeeze the softened gelatine to remove excess water, then add it to the hot cream mixture, stirring until completely dissolved.
4. Strain the mixture through a fine sieve into a jug, then pour into 4 glasses or small ramekins. Allow to cool to room temperature, then cover and chill in the refrigerator for at least 4 hours, or overnight, until softly set and gently wobbly.
5. For the figs, preheat the oven to 160°C fan (350°F), Gas Mark 4. In a shallow baking dish, whisk together the melted butter, honey and chopped rosemary. Add the quartered figs and turn to coat. Roast for 10–15 minutes, until the figs are tender and the juices syrupy, basting with the pan juices halfway. Leave to cool to just warm or room temperature.
6. Remove the pannacottas from the refrigerator 20–30 minutes before serving so they lose their chill. Spoon the honeyed figs and their juices over each pannacotta and serve.

LINGUINE PUTTANESCA with crunchy pangrattato

SERVES 4

Bold, salty and full of character, this comes together in minutes from store cupboard ingredients. This recipe uses sweet, silky tomato passata – though you could use canned chopped tomatoes with a tablespoon of tomato pureé – anchovies, capers and olives for that classic, punchy sauce, then a bright, crunchy lemon pangrattato is scattered over the top. The pangrattato soaks up the garlicky oil and adds a lovely toasted texture and freshness that lift the whole dish. It's the kind of recipe you can make on a weeknight, but also happily serve to friends with a glass of red wine... yum!

For the pasta

400g (14oz) linguine
4 tablespoons olive oil
4 garlic cloves, crushed
5 anchovy fillets, finely chopped
2 teaspoons chilli flakes, or to taste
400ml (14fl oz) tomato passata
2 tablespoons capers, rinsed
24 black olives, pitted and roughly chopped
Large handful of basil leaves
Sea salt and freshly ground black pepper

For the lemon pangrattato

4 tablespoons olive oil
1 garlic clove, finely chopped or grated
80g (2¾oz) fresh coarse breadcrumbs, or crumbled stale bread
Finely grated zest of 1 lemon, or more to taste

1 Bring a large pot of well-salted water to the boil. Add the linguine and cook for about 10 minutes until tender. Before draining, scoop out about ½ cup of the pasta-cooking water and set aside.

2 Meanwhile, make the pangrattato. Warm the oil in a small frying pan over a medium heat. Add the garlic and cook for 30 seconds, then stir in the breadcrumbs and a small pinch of salt. Cook, stirring often, for 3–5 minutes until golden and crisp. Take off the heat and stir in the lemon zest.

3 For the sauce, place a wide frying pan over a medium heat and add the olive oil. Add the garlic, anchovies and chilli flakes and cook gently for 1–2 minutes, stirring, until the anchovies start to melt and everything smells fragrant. Pour in the passata with a pinch each of salt and pepper. Let it bubble gently for 5–8 minutes, stirring now and then, until slightly thickened and glossy.

4 Stir in the capers and olives and cook for another minute. Add the drained linguine straight into the pan with the sauce, along with a splash of the reserved pasta-cooking water. Toss everything together over a low heat for a minute or so until the pasta is well coated and the sauce clings to it, adding a little more pasta-cooking water if needed.

5 Taste and adjust the seasoning, then tear in most of the basil and toss once more. Divide between 4 warmed bowls and generously scatter the lemon pangrattato and remaining basil over just before serving, offering the rest in a bowl on the side so people can top up their plates as they eat.

HOT CHOCOLATE AFFOGATO with candied orange peel

SERVES 4

This feels impossibly glamorous for something so quick and easy. My version is rich and dark, with a whisper of orange, hot espresso and chocolate poured at the table over scoops of very cold vanilla ice cream so it melts into a silky, grown-up sundae. I like to serve the sauce in a warmed jug, with the ice cream already in pretty glasses on saucers, so everyone can pour their own at the last moment. It's fabulous for Christmas, but honestly it works at any time of year when you want a dessert that feels special with almost no effort. You can keep the orange, or swap it for other flavours such as coffee, hazelnut or mint to suit the season, as suggested below.

200ml (7fl oz) double cream
200g (7oz) 70 per cent cocoa solids chocolate, chopped, or chocolate chips
100ml (3½fl oz) strong espresso coffee
Finely grated zest of 1 orange
8 scoops of good-quality vanilla ice cream
8 strips of candied orange peel

Clodagh's favourite flavours:

For Christmas, keep the orange zest in the recipe and add 1 tablespoon Grand Marnier or Cointreau for a lovely festive note.

For a deeper coffee flavour, add 1 tablespoon coffee liqueur, such as Kahlúa or Tia Maria.

For a nutty twist, use 1 tablespoon Frangelico and top with a few chopped toasted hazelnuts.

For summer, leave out the orange zest and add a few drops of peppermint extract, or finish with a few raspberries, for a brighter feel.

1 Chill 4 heatproof glasses or serving dishes. Gently warm a heatproof serving jug in a low oven, or with a rinse of hot water, drying it well.

2 Place the cream, chocolate, espresso and orange zest in a small saucepan over a low heat. Stir slowly until the chocolate has fully melted and the mixture is smooth and glossy. If using a liqueur or peppermint extract, stir it in at the end and taste, adjusting to your liking. Keep the sauce over the lowest heat, or turn off the heat and cover to keep warm.

3 Place 2 scoops of vanilla ice cream into each chilled glass or cup and set them on saucers with a spoon and 2 strips of candied orange peel on the side.

4 Pour the hot chocolate sauce into the warmed jug and bring it to the table with the ice cream glasses or cups. In front of your guests, pour the hot chocolate and espresso sauce over the ice cream so it begins to melt and ripple, then place 2 strips of candied orange peel on top of each. Serve immediately.

taste

CHEESE SOUFFLÉ

SERVES 4

This fabulous soufflé looks so impressive: puffed and golden in a big dish so everyone can dive in and serve themselves spoonfuls of hot, airy cheese. It feels theatrical, but the method is simple. It's great for parties or as a fun family supper; just add a big green salad. The first time I had this was at my great friend Louise Fennell's house; she is famous for it and makes it effortlessly. I was so wowed by it that I spent the following few weeks testing this recipe!

60g (2¼oz) unsalted butter, plus more for the dish
20g (¾oz) dried breadcrumbs
60g (2¼oz) plain flour
560ml (1 pint) whole milk, at room temperature
1 teaspoon Dijon mustard
3 garlic cloves, finely grated or crushed
80g (2¾oz) Gruyère or mature Cheddar, grated
6 eggs, separated
Small bunch of chives, finely chopped
Sea salt and freshly ground black pepper

Clodagh's tips for soufflé success!

Make sure your cheese sauce is only warm (not hot) before you fold in the egg whites, so they don't deflate.

Whisk the whites to firm, glossy peaks, not dry. Fold them into the mix gently, with a light hand.

Have your oven fully preheated and avoid opening the door while it bakes, so the heat stays steady and the soufflé can rise and set properly.

1 Generously butter a 22cm (8½-inch) soufflé dish. Add the breadcrumbs and rotate the dish to coat the base and sides evenly, then tap out any excess. Set aside.

2 Melt the butter in a saucepan over a low heat. Add the flour and stir until smooth, then cook for 2 minutes, stirring. Slowly whisk in the milk, a little at a time, whisking until you have a smooth, glossy sauce. Whisk in the mustard and garlic. Simmer very gently over a low heat, stirring often, for 3–4 minutes until it thickens and coats the back of a spoon. Season well, then leave to cool for about 15 minutes until just warm. Preheat the oven to 180°C fan (400°F), Gas Mark 6. Place a large baking tray on the middle shelf to heat up.

3 Fold in the cheese until melted and evenly distributed. Stir the egg yolks into the warm (not hot) cheese sauce, one at a time, until fully combined.

4 In a clean, dry bowl, whisk the egg whites with a pinch of salt to stiff peaks. Add a large spoon of egg white to the cheese mixture and stir to loosen. Fold in the chives, then gently fold in the remaining egg whites in 2–3 additions, using a large spoon and taking care not to knock out too much air. Pour into the dish, filling it to 2–3cm (1 inch) from the top. Smooth the surface, then run the tip of a knife around the inside of the dish to help it rise.

5 Set the soufflé dish on the preheated baking tray and close the oven door quickly. Bake for 25–30 minutes, until well risen, golden on top and with a slight wobble in the centre. Serve immediately, taking it straight to the table for everyone to enjoy at its peak.

STEAK with Cognac pepper sauce

SERVES 4

This feels so luxurious, yet it's one of the easiest, most satisfying dishes you can make at home. When you're buying steak, look for well-marbled fillet with a deep colour, a dry surface and pieces that are an even thickness so they cook at the same pace. The inspiration comes from one of my favourite Paris bistros, Le Bistrot Paul Bert, where Harry and I love to sneak away for weekends on our own. If you don't have Cognac, use Armagnac, Madeira or Marsala; each brings its own character to the rich, velvety sauce that is so good with skinny fries.

For the steaks

4 filet mignon steaks
2 tablespoons black peppercorns
2 tablespoons flavourless oil, such as sunflower
80g (2¾oz) unsalted butter
Sea salt flakes

For the Cognac pepper sauce

150ml (¼ pint) Cognac, plus 1 teaspoon, to taste
150ml (¼ pint) beef stock (for homemade, see page 64)
200ml (7fl oz) double cream

Clodagh's cooking times for super steaks:

These timings are for steaks 3cm / 1¼-inches thick). For thinner steaks (about 2cm / ¾-inch thick), reduce the time you cook them on each side by about 1 minute.

Rare: 2–3 minutes per side
Medium-rare: 3–4 minutes per side
Medium: 4–5 minutes per side

1 Remove the steaks from the refrigerator 30–40 minutes before cooking to come to room temperature. Pat dry with kitchen paper and season both sides lightly with sea salt flakes. Coarsely crush the peppercorns using a mortar and pestle, or bash them in a bag with a rolling pin. Press the crushed pepper firmly on to both sides of each steak to form a generous crust.

2 Heat a heavy frying pan over a medium-high heat until very hot. Add the oil and butter. When the butter foams, lay in the steaks and sear for 2–3 minutes on each side for rare, or see my timings above, depending on thickness. Turn them only once for a good crust. Transfer to a warm plate, tent loosely with foil and leave to rest. Pour off any excess fat from the pan, but leave the browned bits in the bottom; they give great flavour.

3 Take the pan off the heat for a moment, then carefully pour in the Cognac. Return to a medium heat and let it reduce until almost syrupy, scraping up those browned bits. Stir in the stock and simmer for 2–3 minutes until reduced by half. Reduce the heat, pour in the cream and bubble gently for a few minutes until thickened and glossy. Taste and adjust the seasoning and, if you like, add an extra teaspoon of Cognac off the heat for more fragrance.

4 Serve the rested steaks on warmed plates, then spoon on the sauce generously, or serve it alongside in a jug. Serve with skinny fries and dressed green salad for that bistro-at-home feeling.

15-MINUTE FRENCH CHOCOLATE MOUSSE

SERVES 4

One of the most delicious and easiest dinner party desserts, these take fifteen minutes to prepare, can be made a day ahead and feel instantly special when you serve them in your prettiest glasses. The silky, dark mousse can be kept simple or gently perfumed with rose, orange or coffee. Make them ahead, stack them on a tray in the refrigerator and bring to the table finished with a drizzle of extra virgin olive oil (it's amazing, trust me) and a sprinkle of sea salt flakes, for an effortless, very French end to the meal. I love to tie thin ribbons around the stems of the glasses; it looks so chic.

100g (3½oz) 70 per cent cocoa solids chocolate, chopped
60g (2¼oz) caster sugar
2 large eggs, at room temperature
250g (9oz) mascarpone

Optional flavourings (choose one):
1 tablespoon rose water
1 tablespoon orange liqueur, such as Cointreau, and the finely grated zest of ½ orange
1 tablespoon strong espresso, cooled

Clodagh's marvellous mousse-serving tips:
Classic: A drizzle of extra virgin olive oil and a sprinkling of sea salt flakes.
Rose water: Top with a few raspberries and a light scattering of chopped pistachios.
Orange: Add more finely grated orange zest on top and a few curls of dark chocolate.
Coffee: Finish with a dusting of cocoa powder or finely grated dark chocolate and a single coffee bean on each.

1 Place the chopped dark chocolate in a heatproof bowl set over a saucepan of barely simmering water, making sure the bowl does not touch the water. Leave to melt gently, stirring once or twice, then remove from the heat and let cool for 2–3 minutes.

2 Stir the sugar into the warm chocolate until dissolved, then add the eggs and your chosen flavouring, if using. With a handheld electric whisk, beat the mixture for 4–5 minutes, until it thickens slightly, looks glossy and has increased a little in volume. Add the mascarpone and whisk briefly, just until smoothly combined; take care not to over-beat at this stage, so the mixture stays light.

3 Divide between 4 small glasses or dessert cups. Cover and chill in the refrigerator for at least 15 minutes, or up to 24 hours, until softly set.

4 Just before serving, you can finish each mousse with a drizzle of extra virgin olive oil and a sprinkling of sea salt flakes; or a few raspberries and pistachios; chocolate curls and orange zest; or cocoa and coffee beans, depending on whether you've chosen to serve it flavoured or not. Or, of course, completely unadorned! It'll still be delicious.

HALF A PINT OF PRAWNS & HOMEMADE MAYONNAISE

SERVES 8

One of those starters that always makes me smile, because it's all about simple pleasures and a bit of theatre. At our little pub, I love serving these prawns in old traditional half-pint glasses, all gathered on a tray along the bar, with a big bowl of homemade mayonnaise in the middle. People just help themselves, picking up a glass and scooping the prawns straight through the mayonnaise, and it instantly feels like you are in a pub in Ireland. It's the most effortless starter to put together, but somehow it always feels so special. And don't be daunted by the quantities, because this is super-easy to scale up or down, as you prefer.

1kg (2lb 4oz) raw king prawns, tails on
Sea salt
Lemon wedges, to serve

For the mayonnaise
4 egg yolks
2 teaspoons Dijon mustard
2 tablespoons white wine vinegar
200ml (7fl oz) extra virgin olive oil
200ml (7fl oz) vegetable oil

1. Bring a large pot of water to the boil and add a good sprinkle of sea salt. Drop the prawns into the salted boiling water and cook for 4 minutes; once cooked, the prawns change from grey to pink. Drain and allow to cool.
2. Now for the mayonnaise. Put the yolks into a bowl, followed by the mustard, vinegar and a pinch of salt. Measure out both the oils into a jug and whisk them into the egg yolks in a very thin stream. The mayonnaise will begin to become thick and creamy as more oil is added. When it's all added, spoon into a bowl.
3. Serve the mayonnaise with the prawns in half-pint jars, with lemon wedges for squeezing.

PUB LUNCH PIE!
with chicken & tarragon

SERVES 8

Some recipes feel like they belong to a particular place, and for me, this pie is for a long, lazy lunch in our little pub in the woods. The pastry is golden and crisp, the filling rich with chicken and herbs, and it's the kind of dish that invites everyone to linger by the fire with another glass of wine.

For the filling
1 litre (1¾ pints) chicken stock
2 bay leaves
1 teaspoon black peppercorns
3 thyme sprigs
2 rosemary sprigs
10 skinless chicken thighs
2 leeks, thickly sliced
80g (2¾oz) unsalted butter
80g (2¾oz) plain flour
50ml (1¾fl oz) double cream
2 tablespoons English mustard
50g (1¾oz) Cheddar, grated
300g (10½oz) flaked ham
2 tablespoons finely chopped flat leaf parsley leaves
Sea salt and freshly ground white pepper

For the pastry
Plain flour, to dust
2 ready-rolled all-butter shortcrust pastry sheets (or for homemade, double the recipe on page 53)
1 egg yolk, lightly beaten

1 Pour the stock into a large saucepan and add the bay leaves, peppercorns, thyme and rosemary. Bring to a simmer for 5 minutes to infuse. Add the chicken and return to a gentle simmer for 25 minutes, until cooked. Add the leeks and cook for 10–15 minutes, until soft. Set a sieve over a large heatproof bowl and drain the chicken and leeks, reserving the stock. Discard the herbs and peppercorns. Shred the chicken into bite-sized pieces.

2 In a clean large saucepan, melt the butter over a medium-low heat. Stir in the flour and cook for 1 minute. Swap to a whisk and gradually pour in 600ml of the reserved hot stock, whisking until you have a smooth sauce. Cook over a medium-low heat for 2–3 minutes, stirring, until thickened and bubbling gently. Remove from the heat, then stir in the cream, mustard and Cheddar until the cheese has melted. Season to taste with salt and white pepper. Fold in the shredded chicken, leeks and flaked ham. Transfer to a large bowl and leave to cool, then stir through the parsley. Cover and refrigerate until cold.

3 Lightly flour a work surface. Roll out a sheet of pastry, if needed, to fit a 23cm (9-inch) pie tin about 5cm (2 inches) deep. Line the tin with the pastry, pressing it gently into the corners and up the sides. Leave a little overhang and brush the rim with beaten egg yolk.

4 Roll out the second sheet of pastry to form a lid. Spoon the chilled filling into the tin. Lay the lid over and seal the edges, trimming off excess (use this to make 'leaves'). Attach the decorations with egg yolk, then brush the pie all over and cut a hole in the top for steam to escape. Chill for 30 minutes. Preheat the oven to 190°C fan (410°F), Gas Mark 6½.

5 Bake for 35–45 minutes, until deep golden and crisp. Set aside for 10 minutes, then serve.

BLACKBERRY & LEMON CHEESECAKE with buttery pecan biscuit base

SERVES 8

Late summer is the perfect moment for this cheesecake, when wild hedgerows are heavy with sun-warmed blackberries. A buttery pecan and digestive biscuit base carries a cool, lemon-bright cream cheese filling, finished with a glossy tumble of just-cooked blackberries. It's rich yet refreshing, with citrus cutting through the sweetness and the berries bringing that nostalgic, just-picked flavour. Make it ahead for effortless end-of-summer suppers, when you want something that feels both a little wild and a bit luxurious. You can swap out blackberries for other fruits throughout the year, such as raspberries, gooseberries, sliced peaches or figs.

For the base

250g (9oz) digestive biscuits

80g (2¾oz) pecans

150g (5½oz) unsalted butter, melted

For the filling

300ml (½ pint) double cream

150g (5½oz) caster sugar

340g (11¾oz) cream cheese

Finely grated zest of 3 lemons, plus the juice of 2 lemons

For the blackberry layer

450–500g (1lb–1lb 2oz) fresh blackberries, or frozen, defrosted and well drained

2–3 tablespoons caster sugar, to taste

1 tablespoon lemon juice

1. Line the base of an 18cm (7-inch) springform cake tin with baking parchment.
2. Put the biscuits and pecans in a food processor and blitz to a fine crumb. Add the melted butter and pulse-blend until starting to clump. Tip into the prepared tin, pressing it firmly and evenly over the base with the back of a spoon. Chill in the refrigerator while you make the filling.
3. Whip the double cream to soft peaks. Add the caster sugar, cream cheese, lemon zest and juice and whip again until thick, smooth and light; it should hold its shape.
4. Spoon the lemon mixture over the chilled biscuit base. Smooth the top and return to the refrigerator for at least 2 hours, or until set.
5. Make the blackberry layer. Place the berries in a small saucepan with the sugar and lemon juice. Warm gently until the berries release their juices. Remove from the heat and cool completely.
6. Once the cheesecake filling is set and the blackberry mixture is cool, strain the blackberries and transfer the juice to a jug to serve with the cheesecake. Spoon the berries over the filling in an even layer. Chill for a further 30–60 minutes to let the topping settle.
7. Remove from the refrigerator 30 minutes before serving, to allow to return to room temperature. Serve with the jug of blackberry juice.

The Cork Arms
Our Little Pub in the Woods

The Cork Arms began as a half-joke and a quiet dream on a walk through the woods. For years, every time we passed that fallen-down shed with its listing walls and collapsed roof, I would turn to Harry and say, 'One day I'd love to turn that into a little pub.' He would gently shuttle me along with a doubtful, 'I don't think so,' and the trees would swallow the idea again.

Life moved on, the seasons turned and the shed stayed as it was, quietly waiting in the undergrowth. When we started planning our wedding, the dream came back in a more practical – and urgent – way. I was trawling through options for marquees for the after-party, looking at the eye-watering cost of something so temporary as well as thinking about the energy and resources it would devour. It felt wrong to put up a structure for a single night and then watch it vanish. Somewhere in that frustration, the idea of the Irish pub resurfaced. I missed that local pub feeling I'd known from when I lived in Ireland: the warmth, the familiarity, the sense of a place that is always there, ready to welcome you in. Instead of hiring a marquee, I became determined to restore the shed and turn it into my own version of an Irish pub, sitting permanently in the woods.

By then, we had been seasoning wood from fallen trees in the woodland at Broadspear, quietly building up a stash of timber with real character. The Cork Arms was rebuilt almost entirely from that seasoned wood, so the building is literally made from the landscape that surrounds it. The bar counter you see when you walk in came from a tree that was struck by lightning and had to be felled, which broke our hearts because it stood right in front of the Walled Garden. We seasoned it, cherished it and turned it into the centrepiece of the pub, so it lives on forever as the place everyone naturally leans against with a drink in hand.

From the start, I wanted the Cork Arms to feel utterly authentic, as if it had somehow always been there. Little shelves were built into the gaps between the wooden supports and along the walls, perfectly sized for bottles behind the bar and for pictures collected over time. As they filled up, they gave the space that familiar, layered feeling of a well-loved pub, where every shelf has a history and every frame holds a memory. A log burner with a tall chimney heats the room, fed with wood and kindling from the farm, so on cold evenings the pub becomes a warm cocoon in the trees, powered by the land itself. Comfort was as important as atmosphere. To the left as you walk in, I created a cosy snug: an old Chesterfield from eBay, a couple of armchairs, shelves laden with books and musical instruments scattered around. It's a tiny sitting room within the pub, perfect for music sessions with friends or wintry afternoons when the fire is lit and someone curls up with a book. On the right-hand side is a small kitchen and dining table, so we can have lunches and dinners there. The cupboards are built from the remains of an old gate, tying the space back to the farm's past.

Slowly, The Cork Arms moved from being a rescued shed to the centre of our celebrations. It was baptised on our wedding night, and since then, birthdays, Christmases, New Years, harvest suppers and summer barbecues have all gravitated there. The biggest night of all is our St Patrick's Day party, a massive celebration of my heritage: Irish stew bubbling away, platters of oysters, slices of Guinness cake, musicians squeezed into the snug, sing-songs that spill out into the woods and, sometimes, Irish dancing on the bar counter itself. On those nights, with the fire blazing, the shelves glowing with bottles and the music echoing through the trees, The Cork Arms feels exactly as I had imagined on those early walks: a tiny, magical Irish pub in the heart of Broadspear.

Our pub pre-renovation, October 2020

Summer barbecue, August 2023

Christmas at the pub, 2025

Summer party buffet, June 2024

June 2023

Harry and his Guinness, May 2022

The first pint of Guinness we served, August 2021

The bar counter made from a fallen oak tree

Theo Fennell and Imelda May, St Patrick's Day 2023

LEMONY RASPBERRY POSSETS

SERVES 4

Lemon posset is one of those brilliant, effortless desserts that feels far more elegant than you'd know from the work involved. This version takes just 15 minutes to prepare, can be made a day ahead, and is layered with raspberries both folded through the silky lemon cream and spooned over the top just before serving. The sharpness of the lemon and the sweetness of the berries are such a perfect match and the whole makes a delicious palate cleanser.

Finely grated zest of 2 lemons, plus 100ml (3½fl oz) lemon juice (from about 2 lemons), plus lemon slices (optional), to serve
100g (3½oz) caster sugar
500ml (18fl oz) double cream
150g (5½oz) raspberries, plus more to serve
A few small mint leaves, to serve (optional)

Clodagh's perfect possets:
Blackberries for a deeper, more autumnal flavour.
Blueberries for a softer, sweeter finish.
Strawberries, finely chopped, in summer.
Poached rhubarb for a beautiful sharpness in spring (see page 59).

1. Place the lemon zest and juice and sugar in a saucepan and place over a low heat. Stir until the sugar has dissolved, then pour in the cream. Bring to a gentle boil, then reduce the heat slightly and simmer for 3 minutes, stirring often. Remove from the heat and leave to cool for 5 minutes.
2. Gently fold 100g (3½oz) of the raspberries through the warm lemon cream, taking care not to crush them too much. Divide between 4 small glasses or bowls and chill for 1 hour.
3. After 1 hour in the refrigerator, spoon the remaining raspberries over the top of each posset and gently press them in, so they are half submerged. Return to the refrigerator and chill for at least 2 hours, or overnight, until softly set.
4. Serve well chilled and set, with lemon slices and mint leaves, if you like.

GOOEY CHOCOLATE PUDDINGS with roasted hazlenuts

SERVES 6

Everything a chocolate dessert should be: warm, gooey and just a little bit indulgent, yet wonderfully simple. I love baking these in old china cups to serve on their saucers, looking so pretty and a bit fun, but still perfectly robust for the oven. You can mix the batter earlier in the day, spoon it into the nut-lined cups and chill for a few hours, then simply pop them into the oven as you clear the main course, baking until the tops are just set and the centres soft and molten.

30g (1oz) unsalted butter, plus more for the cups
100g (3½oz) blanched hazelnuts, very finely chopped
180g (6oz) 70 per cent cocoa solids chocolate, broken into pieces
4 eggs, separated
100g (3½oz) caster sugar
50g (1¾oz) plain flour
Sea salt flakes, to serve (optional)

Optional flavour twists (choose one):
1 tablespoon strong coffee or espresso, cooled
1 tablespoon orange liqueur, such as Cointreau, and the finely grated zest of ½ orange
1 tablespoon Frangelico, or other liqueur

1. Preheat the oven to 160°C fan (350°F), Gas Mark 4. Generously butter 6 ovenproof china cups or small ramekins. Sprinkle about half the hazelnuts around the inside of each cup, turning them so the nuts lightly coat the base and sides. Tip out any excess and reserve for the topping.
2. Place the dark chocolate in a heatproof bowl set over a saucepan of barely simmering water, making sure the bowl does not touch the water. Leave to melt gently, stirring once or twice, then remove from the heat and allow to cool slightly.
3. Meanwhile, whisk the egg yolks and sugar in a bowl until pale and slightly thickened. Stir in the remaining chopped hazelnuts and your chosen flavouring, if using. Pour in the chocolate and whisk until smooth, then sift in the flour and fold it through until just combined.
4. In a clean, dry bowl, whisk the egg whites to stiff peaks. Stir a large spoon of egg white into the chocolate to loosen it, then gently fold in the rest in 2–3 additions, taking care not to knock out too much air. Divide between the cups or ramekins, filling them about three-quarters full. You can chill these now, or if cooking immediately, place the cups on a baking tray and bake for 9–10 minutes, until the tops are just set but the centres still feel soft when you gently shake the tray.
5. Serve immediately, on saucers, with a jug of cream, a scoop of vanilla ice cream (Harry's favourite) or spoon of crème fraîche alongside, and the reserved hazelnuts and sea salt flakes sprinkled over.

Gatherings

Menu

St Patrick's Day

Irish Spring Green Soup

Cheddar-Thyme Soda Scones

Seville Marmalade Ham
with Parsley Sauce

Buttery Colcannon

Guinness Cake

IRISH SPRING GREEN SOUP

SERVES 6

Every St Patrick's Day, this is the soup that welcomes everyone to The Cork Arms. I make it in my biggest pot (usually scaling this recipe up by four or five times) and set it up on the bar with a stack of cups beside it, a bowl of cool crème fraîche and little dishes of chopped herbs, so guests can add what they want. Sometimes I add bowls of toasted sesame, pumpkin or sunflower seeds, hazelnuts or almonds, or finely chopped spring onions, too, for a bit of crunch and bite. It's bright, light and incredibly good for you – full of peas, spinach, spring greens and herbs – but still feels cosy and comforting in the way only a warm soup can. I love how unapologetically green it is; it looks beautifully Irish in the cup, tastes like the very first days of spring, and is especially delicious served alongside my Cheddar-Thyme Soda Scones (see opposite).

40g (1½oz) unsalted butter
1½ tablespoons olive oil, plus more (optional) to serve
6 spring onions, or 1 leek, finely sliced
3 garlic cloves, finely sliced
1 large floury potato, peeled and finely chopped
1.2 litres (2 pints) hot vegetable stock (for homemade, see page 125), or light chicken stock, plus more if needed
225g (8oz) peas (fresh or frozen and defrosted)
150g (5½oz) baby spinach
150g (5½oz) spring greens, or young cabbage, finely shredded
Handful of parsley leaves, plus more (optional) to serve
Handful of mint leaves, plus more (optional) to serve
Squeeze of lemon juice
Sea salt and freshly ground black pepper
Crème fraîche, to serve (optional)

1. Warm the butter and olive oil in a saucepan over a medium-low heat. Add the spring onions or leek, garlic and a pinch of salt, then cook gently for 10 minutes until softened but not coloured.
2. Stir in the potato and cook for 2 minutes, then pour in the hot stock. Bring to a simmer and cook for about 10 minutes, until the potato is just tender.
3. Add the peas, spinach and shredded greens. Simmer for 2–3 minutes only, until the leaves have just wilted and everything is a bright, vivid green.
4. Take off the heat and add the parsley and mint. Blend the soup straight away with a stick blender, or in a jug blender, until completely smooth and silky; this helps keep the colour bright.
5. Return to the pan, loosen with a splash more stock or hot water if needed, and season with salt, pepper and a squeeze of lemon juice to lift the flavours. Serve hot in warmed bowls, with crème fraîche or good olive oil and a few more herbs on top, if you like.

CHEDDAR-THYME SODA SCONES

MAKES 12

I love the aroma of scones or bread baking in the oven, wafting through our home... I find it's the most welcoming fragrance, it truly makes me happy. These scones are everything I love about savoury baking: quick to pull together, deeply comforting and endlessly useful. They take just a few minutes to mix and the dough is simply patted out and cut: no faff, no special equipment. The sharp mature Cheddar, thyme and little hit of mustard bake into scones with a golden, cheesy crust and a soft, tender middle. They're delicious warm from the oven on their own, but just as good dipped into a bowl of soup, or split and piled with cheese and chutney. I often make a double batch and freeze some, ready for last-minute lunches.

380g (13oz) plain flour, plus more to dust
2 teaspoons bicarbonate of soda
50g (1¾oz) unsalted butter, chopped
240g (8½oz) mature Cheddar, grated
1 tablespoon chopped thyme leaves
1 egg
1 teaspoon Dijon mustard
260ml (9½fl oz) buttermilk
Sea salt flakes

1. Preheat the oven to 180°C fan (400°F), Gas Mark 6. Line a large baking tray with baking parchment.
2. Sift the flour and bicarbonate of soda into a large mixing bowl. Rub the butter into the flour mixture until it resembles fine crumbs. Stir in two-thirds of the grated cheese, followed by half the thyme.
3. Whisk together the egg, mustard and buttermilk in a jug. Make a well in the centre of the floury crumbs and gradually pour in the buttermilk mixture, using a fork to bring it together into a soft dough. Keep a bit of the liquid back for glazing the scones.
4. Roll out the dough on a lightly floured work surface to a thickness of 2cm (¾ inch). Cut into circles with a pastry cutter or upturned glass and place on the prepared tray. Brush with the remaining buttermilk mix, then sprinkle the remaining cheese and thyme on top with some sea salt flakes.
5. Bake in the preheated oven for 12–15 minutes, then transfer to a wire rack to cool.

SEVILLE MARMALADE HAM with parsley sauce

SERVES 6–8

The glowing centrepiece of my St Patrick's Day celebrations; I make it for our annual party in our little pub at Broadspear, The Cork Arms (see page 182). It makes me emotional every time I cook it, as my mum made a version for us when I was growing up in Cork, and the smell takes me straight back to her kitchen. The parsley sauce is pure Irish nostalgia: creamy, flecked with herbs and just sharp enough with mustard to cut through the rich ham. It feels celebratory, yet is wonderfully straightforward, and it fills the kitchen with the most irresistible smell.

1 whole gammon (2–2.5kg / 4lb 8oz–5lb 8oz)
1 teaspoon black peppercorns
2 bay leaves
Handful of cloves
1 jar of Seville marmalade

For the parsley sauce
2 tablespoons unsalted butter
1 onion, finely chopped
2 tablespoons plain flour
200ml (7fl oz) whole milk
2 tablespoons finely chopped parsley leaves
1 teaspoon English mustard
Pinch of freshly grated nutmeg
Sea salt and freshly ground black pepper

1. Place the gammon in a large pot and cover with cold water. Add the black peppercorns and tear in the bay leaves. Bring to the boil, then reduce the heat to a simmer and cook for 20 minutes for each 450g (1lb). Skim off any white froth that rises to the surface.
2. Carefully remove the ham from the liquid, reserving 200ml (7fl oz) of it for the sauce, and preheat the oven to 180°C fan (400°F), Gas Mark 6. Using a sharp knife, carefully peel off the outer skin of the meat, leaving a thin layer of white fat underneath. Score the fat in a diamond pattern (be careful not to cut into the meat). Push a whole clove into the centre of each diamond. Spoon the marmalade over the ham.
3. Roast the ham, uncovered, for 40 minutes, basting every 15 minutes. Remove from the oven and leave to rest in a warm place for 15 minutes while you make the sauce.
4. Melt the butter in a saucepan over a medium heat. Stir in the onion and cook for 1 minute. Next, stir in the flour and cook, stirring, for about 1 minute more. Add the reserved cooking liquid slowly, whisking constantly, then add the milk in the same way. When you have a smooth sauce, stir in the parsley, mustard and nutmeg and season with salt and pepper. Continue to whisk until the sauce is smooth. Cook for another 3 minutes, whisking constantly, until it thickens, then serve the sauce with the carved ham.

BUTTERY COLCANNON

SERVES 6

For me, this is the ultimate Irish soul food, the kind of dish that tastes like home, comfort and childhood all in one spoonful. At its heart, it's simply buttery mashed potatoes folded together with something green: most often cabbage, but sometimes spring onions or soft, slow-cooked leeks, depending on the season and what you have. Everyone seems to have their own version and I love them all. I always reach for a good floury potato here, such as Maris Piper or King Edward, so the mash turns out light and fluffy and really soaks up all that butter. One of my all-time favourite ways to eat it is with a thick slice of Seville Marmalade Ham and a spoonful of Parsley Sauce (see opposite)... oh my God, they are so incredible together, the salty-sweet ham and sauce sinking into the buttery potatoes and greens.

1kg (2lb 4oz) floury potatoes, scrubbed
100ml (3½fl oz) whole milk
200g (7oz) cabbage, finely sliced, or spring greens or kale, coarse stems removed
100g (3½oz) unsalted butter, plus more to serve
¼ teaspoon freshly grated nutmeg, plus more to taste
Sea salt and freshly ground black pepper

1. Place the potatoes in a large saucepan, putting the biggest at the bottom. Add enough cold water to just cover, season with a little salt, then cover with a lid and bring to the boil over a high heat. Once boiling, pour off about half the water, leaving just enough for the potatoes to steam. Reduce the heat to a gentle simmer and cook for 30–40 minutes, or until the potatoes are completely tender when pierced with a knife.
2. While the potatoes are cooking, pour the milk into a separate saucepan. Slice the cabbage, greens or kale and add to the milk with the butter, nutmeg and a good pinch each of salt and pepper. Place over a medium heat and bring just up to a simmer, then reduce the heat and cook gently for about 4 minutes, until the greens are soft but still bright in colour. Keep warm over a very low heat.
3. When the potatoes are cooked, drain off any remaining water. Holding each potato in a tea towel, peel off the skins while they are still hot and return the flesh to the warm pan or a large bowl. Mash until smooth.
4. Gradually pour the warm milk, cabbage and butter mixture into the mashed potatoes, beating well until you have a soft, fluffy mash streaked with tender cabbage. Taste and adjust the seasoning with more salt, pepper or a little nutmeg if needed.
5. Serve immediately, with an extra knob of butter melting in the centre of the bowl.

GUINNESS CAKE

MAKES 1 CAKE / SERVES 10–12

My ultimate Guinness cake: dark, moist and deeply chocolatey, with just a gentle bitterness from the stout that keeps it from ever tasting too sweet. The cream cheese icing is piled thickly on top like the head on a pint, and the contrast of tangy, soft white against almost-black cake is irresistible. It's a real showstopper for St Patrick's Day, but I make it all year round for birthdays and big gatherings; it keeps beautifully and somehow tastes even better the next day. It is – and I mean it – the best chocolate cake I have ever tasted…

260g (9½oz) unsalted butter, plus more for the tin
300ml (½ pint) Guinness
100g (3½oz) cocoa powder
2 eggs
420g (15oz) caster sugar
2 teaspoons vanilla extract
180ml (6fl oz) buttermilk
300g (10½oz) plain flour
2 teaspoons bicarbonate of soda
1 teaspoon baking powder

For the icing

100g (3½oz) unsalted butter, softened
300g (10½oz) icing sugar
1 teaspoon vanilla extract
300g (10½oz) full-fat cream cheese

1 Preheat the oven to 170°C fan (375°F), Gas Mark 5. Line the base of a 30cm (12-inch) round springform tin with baking parchment and lightly butter the sides.

2 To make the cake, place the butter in a large saucepan over a medium heat and melt gently. Stir in the Guinness, then remove the pan from the heat and whisk in the cocoa powder until smooth. Set aside to cool slightly.

3 In a large mixing bowl, whisk together the eggs, caster sugar, vanilla extract and buttermilk until well combined. Slowly pour in the warm Guinness mixture, whisking all the time.

4 In a separate bowl, sift together the flour, bicarbonate of soda and baking powder. Using an electric whisk or a balloon whisk, gradually pour the wet mixture into the dry ingredients, whisking until you have a smooth, even batter with no lumps of flour.

5 Pour the batter into the prepared tin and bake for about 45 minutes, or until the cake has risen and a skewer inserted into the centre comes out clean. Leave to cool in the tin for 10–15 minutes, then remove and transfer to a wire rack to cool completely.

6 For the icing, beat the softened butter and icing sugar together with a handheld electric whisk until very pale and fluffy. Add the vanilla and cream cheese and continue to whisk until smooth, thick and spreadable.

7 Place the cake on a serving plate and generously spread the icing over, letting it billow to mimic the head of a pint of Guinness. It will keep in an airtight container for 1 week.

Menu

Easter

Wild Garlic & Almond Broth

Roast Butterflied Lamb
with Salsa Verde

Gratin Dauphinois

Sesame Honey Mustard
Roast Carrots

Chocolate Easter
Nest

WILD GARLIC & ALMOND BROTH

SERVES 6

At Broadspear, we're blessed with a flourishing patch of wild garlic, a soft green carpet threaded with the most elegant white, starry flowers. The leaves are slender and gently drooping, with that unmistakable garlicky perfume when you crush them lightly between your fingers. When you're picking, look for bright, vivid green leaves and buds that are still fresh and perky, avoiding anything yellowing or tough. I always gather a few extra flower heads to bring back to the house: some for this broth, others simply to nestle in a jug on the table.

90g (3¼oz) blanched almonds, whole or flaked, plus more to serve
75g (2¾oz) unsalted butter
1 large onion, finely chopped
525g (1lb 3oz) potatoes, peeled and finely chopped
1.2 litres (2 pints) hot chicken stock, or vegetable stock (for homemade, see page 125)
375g (13oz) wild garlic leaves, plus wild garlic flowers (optional), to serve
¾ teaspoon freshly grated nutmeg
150ml (¼ pint) double cream
Sea salt and freshly ground black pepper
Extra virgin olive oil, to serve

1. Gently toast the 90g (3¼oz) almonds, plus the almonds to serve, in a dry frying pan over a medium-low heat until pale golden and fragrant. Transfer immediately to a plate to cool (so they don't catch), then roughly chop.
2. Place a saucepan over a medium heat and add the butter. When the butter has melted, add the onion and potatoes, stir, cover with a lid and reduce the heat to low. Leave these to sweat for about 10 minutes, stirring occasionally.
3. Pour in the hot stock and the 90g (3¼oz) toasted chopped almonds and bring to a gentle boil. Let the onions and potatoes cook until completely soft, about 15 minutes.
4. Add the wild garlic and nutmeg, stir and cook for 10 minutes. Once the wild garlic leaves are wilted, pour the mixture into a blender and whiz until smooth. You can also use a stick blender. Season with salt and pepper and return to the saucepan.
5. Stir in the cream and place over a medium heat for just 2 minutes, stirring to warm everything through, then ladle into warmed bowls. Drizzle with olive oil and scatter with wild garlic leaves and/or flowers and the remaining toasted chopped almonds, then serve.

ROAST BUTTERFLIED LAMB with salsa verde

SERVES 6–8

I make this every Easter; it has become as much a part of the day as chocolate eggs. I love laying on a big, relaxed lunch, the table crowded with sharing dishes. If the weather behaves, I sometimes carry everything out to a long table in the woods, with firepits glowing and light flickering through the trees; it feels magical. The lamb takes on the sharp, garlicky marinade, cooks quickly until bronzed on the outside and blushing inside, then slices beautifully. A vivid, punchy salsa verde makes every forkful sing. Don't rush the resting time; that 15 minutes under loose foil is what keeps the meat juicy and easy to slice. You can marinate the lamb hours ahead (even overnight) and make your salsa verde in advance; just return it to room temperature and give it a stir before serving. Carve the lamb across the grain into thin slices and taste the salsa just before serving: a pinch of salt, squeeze of lemon juice or splash of vinegar just before taking to the table can really brighten it.

3 tablespoons olive oil
2 tablespoons red wine vinegar
3 garlic cloves, finely sliced
2 tablespoons finely chopped rosemary leaves
1.5kg (3lb 5oz) boned and butterflied leg of lamb
Sea salt and freshly ground black pepper

For the salsa verde
Leaves from 8 basil sprigs
Leaves from 4 flat leaf parsley sprigs
4 garlic cloves
4 anchovy fillets
3 tablespoons capers, drained
2 tablespoons white wine vinegar
180ml (6fl oz) extra virgin olive oil

1. To make the marinade, mix the regular olive oil, red wine vinegar, garlic and rosemary in a bowl. Season generously. Place the lamb in a roasting tin. Rub the marinade all over both sides, making sure it gets into any folds. Leave to sit for 30 minutes at room temperature, so the flavours can penetrate and the lamb loses its chill.
2. When you're ready to roast the meat, preheat the oven to 200°C fan (425°F), Gas Mark 7. Roast the lamb, skin side up, in the hot oven for 25 minutes for medium-rare, or 30 minutes for medium (or a little longer if you prefer it more well cooked).
3. While the lamb is roasting, make the salsa verde. Finely chop the basil, parsley, garlic, anchovies and capers together until they form a rough paste, then scrape into a bowl. Stir in the white wine vinegar and extra virgin olive oil and season to taste.
4. Once the lamb is cooked to your liking, remove from the oven, tent loosely with foil and leave to rest for 15 minutes.
5. Slice the lamb thinly against the grain and arrange on a warmed serving platter. Spoon the salsa verde down the centre if you like, letting it run slightly between the slices, and take the rest to the table in a small bowl for people to add more as they like.

GRATIN DAUPHINOIS

SERVES 6

My ultimate comfort side, I often tuck this into the middle of the table at Easter and watch everyone go back for 'just one more spoonful'... It's endlessly useful beyond roast lamb, too. Serve it with roast chicken and green salad, steak and green beans, or as the star of a simple supper with braised leeks or roast carrots on the side. It also makes an indulgent partner for baked fish or a pile of simply cooked greens when you want something cosy. I love that you can assemble it the day before and store it in the refrigerator, which makes it perfect when you're feeding a crowd.

Butter, for the dish
900g (2lb) floury potatoes, such as King Edward, peeled
300ml (½ pint) double cream
150ml (¼ pint) whole milk
4 garlic cloves, finely grated or crushed
Freshly grated nutmeg
120g (4¼oz) Gruyère, grated
Sea salt and freshly ground black pepper

1 Preheat the oven to 180°C fan (400°F), Gas Mark 6. Lightly butter a medium ovenproof dish.

2 Slice the potatoes very thinly – about the thickness of a coin – using a sharp knife or a mandoline if you have one. Bring a large pan of salted water to the boil, add the potatoes and simmer for 5 minutes, until starting to soften. Drain carefully and leave to steam-dry for a couple of minutes.

3 In a jug or bowl, whisk the cream, milk, garlic, a good pinch of salt, some pepper and ½ teaspoon freshly grated nutmeg. Stir in most of the Gruyère, keeping a small handful back for the top.

4 Layer the potatoes in the prepared dish, overlapping them slightly. Pour over the creamy mixture, then use your hands or the back of a spoon to press the potatoes down so they are completely submerged. Scatter over the remaining Gruyère.

5 Bake for 30–35 minutes, or until tender when pierced with a knife, bubbling and golden. Leave to stand for 5–10 minutes before serving, so the gratin can settle and will slice cleanly.

Great with... Sesame Honey Mustard Roast Carrots

1. *Arrange 1.5kg (3lb 5oz) peeled carrots (cut into 7cm / 3-inch chunks, or left whole if slim) in a roasting tin in a single layer, drizzle with 3 tablespoons olive oil, season well and roast in an oven preheated to 180°C fan (400°F), Gas Mark 6 for 20 minutes until beginning to soften.*

2. *Meanwhile, whisk together 2 tablespoons clear honey, 2 tablespoons Dijon mustard, 1 tablespoon wholegrain mustard, 2 tablespoons soy sauce or tamari, 2 tablespoons toasted sesame oil and 2 crushed garlic cloves, then stir in 1 tablespoon black and white sesame seeds.*

3. *Toss the carrots with the glaze until well coated, then return to the oven for 10–15 minutes, turning once, until tender and caramelized. Taste, adjust the seasoning, then serve on a warmed platter scattered with more sesame seeds and a handful of chopped coriander or parsley leaves.*

CHOCOLATE EASTER NEST

MAKES 1 CAKE / SERVES 10–12

A real wow! cake, the kind that makes everyone stop and stare when you bring it to the table.

For the cake
170g (5¾oz) soft unsalted butter, plus more for the tin
250g (9oz) caster sugar
4 eggs
330g (11½oz) plain flour
1 teaspoon baking powder
1 teaspoon bicarbonate of soda
70g (2½oz) cocoa powder
370ml (13fl oz) whole milk, at room temperature
1 teaspoon vanilla extract
Fine sea salt

For the chocolate frosting
150g (5½oz) unsalted butter, softened
400g (14oz) icing sugar, sifted
1 teaspoon vanilla extract
100g (3½oz) cocoa powder
400g (14oz) full-fat cream cheese, chilled

For the chocolate nest
300g (10½oz) dark chocolate, melted and cooled slightly
240g (8½oz) mini chocolate eggs

1. Preheat the oven to 180°C fan (400°F), Gas Mark 6. Butter the sides of a 30cm (12-inch) cake tin and line the base with baking parchment. In a large bowl, beat the butter and sugar until very light and fluffy. Add the eggs one at a time, beating well between each and scraping down the sides of the bowl. In a separate bowl, sift together the flour, baking powder, bicarbonate of soda and cocoa with a good pinch of fine sea salt. In a jug, mix the milk and vanilla. Add one-third of the dry ingredients to the butter mixture and beat on low speed until combined, then add one-third of the milk mixture. Repeat, until everything is incorporated and you have a smooth, thick batter. Do not overmix.
2. Pour into the prepared tin and tap gently on the counter to release air bubbles. Bake for 45–50 minutes, or until risen and a skewer inserted into the centre comes out with a few moist crumbs: it should be cooked through but still fudgy. Leave to cool for 10 minutes, then turn out on to a wire rack, peel off the parchment and leave to cool completely.
3. Meanwhile, make the frosting. In a large bowl, beat the butter, icing sugar and vanilla until pale and fluffy. Add the cocoa and beat again. Add the cream cheese and beat just until smooth and thick. Chill in the refrigerator for 20–30 minutes to firm up slightly before icing the cake. For the chocolate 'twigs', line 2–3 baking trays with baking parchment. Using a spoon or piping bag, drizzle the melted chocolate in thin, criss-cross lines into twig shapes, some long and some short. Chill for at least 15 minutes, until set and crisp.
4. Place the cake on a serving plate. Using a palette knife, spread the frosting over the top and sides, smoothing or swirling. Add an extra mound of frosting in the centre. Pile the mini chocolate eggs into the centre, building them up into a high mound. Carefully peel the chocolate twigs off the paper and arrange them around the eggs to create a nest.

Menu

Summer Garden Party

STARTERS

Chilled Cucumber Consommé

Summer Crudité Platter
with Creamy Feta-Herb Dip

Super-fun Prawn Cocktails

BARBECUE

The Best Burgers

Tuscan Barbecue Chicken

Sticky Harissa Honey Ribs

Charred Corn on the Cob
with Lime, Chilli & Parmesan

Menu

Summer Garden Party

SALADS

Three Bean Salad with Corn, Peppers & Lime

Summer Potato Salad with Peas & Radishes

Crunchy Apple Slaw

Carrot, Raisin & Almond Salad with Mint & Coriander

DESSERT

Lemon Jelly

CHILLED CUCUMBER CONSOMMÉ

SERVES 8

For my big garden party, I always like to start with something cool and fresh that people can sip as they wander and chat, so this chilled soup is perfect. I serve it in little glasses on trays, dressed with colourful herbs so it looks as fabulous as it tastes. I make it with the cucumbers we grow, which are so fresh and crisp; and when they come, they come fast and in abundance, so this is a lovely way to celebrate them. The best part is you can make the soup a couple of days in advance and keep it in jugs in the refrigerator, ready to pour; just give it a really good stir before you fill the glasses and take them out into the garden.

6 cucumbers, thinly sliced
330g (11½oz) Greek yogurt
Leaves from a small bunch of basil
80ml (2¾fl oz) extra virgin olive oil, plus more to serve
3 tablespoons lemon juice, or to taste
2 tablespoons chopped dill
1 garlic clove, finely grated or crushed
½ teaspoon clear honey, or to taste
Sea salt and freshly ground black pepper
Mint leaves, dill or chives, or cucumber or borage flowers, to serve

1. Place the cucumbers, Greek yogurt, basil, olive oil, lemon juice, dill, garlic and honey in a blender. Add a generous pinch of salt and several grinds of pepper.
2. Blend on high until completely smooth and silky. Taste and adjust the seasoning, adding a little more salt, lemon juice or honey if needed.
3. Transfer to a jug or bowl, cover and chill in the refrigerator for at least 4 hours, or until very cold. It can happily be made the day before. Chill the bowls or glasses to serve it in, too.
4. When ready to serve, give the soup a stir, then pour into the chilled bowls or glasses. Finish with a drizzle of olive oil, a few herb leaves, cucumber or borage flowers if you have them, and an extra grind of pepper.

SUMMER CRUDITÉ PLATTER with creamy feta-herb dip

SERVES 4–6 AS A STARTER OR A SNACK

On warm days, this is exactly the sort of thing I love to put in the middle of the table: a big platter of crisp, colourful vegetables with a cool, creamy dip that tastes like the garden. The feta and yogurt make it tangy and light, while soft herbs and peppery rocket bring a fresh green flavour that works with almost anything you're picking. It takes only minutes to blend together and looks so pretty topped with chopped nuts and seeds, ready for everyone to scoop and dip. If you have other herbs to hand – basil, parsley or tarragon – you can easily fold those in too, so the dip changes to include whatever is at its best. This easily scales up, for a larger group.

For the dip

150g (5½oz) feta
Finely grated zest and juice of 1 lemon
100ml (3½fl oz) extra virgin olive oil, plus more to serve
100g (3½oz) natural yogurt
1 tablespoon chopped soft herbs, such as mint leaves, dill and chives
2 tablespoons rocket leaves
2–3 tablespoons finely chopped mixed nuts and seeds, such as pistachios, almonds, pumpkin seeds and sunflower seeds
Sea salt and freshly ground black pepper

For the crudités

Use a mix of what is best and freshest, such as:
Baby carrots, trimmed and halved lengthways
Cucumber or celery, cut into batons
Baby courgettes and their flowers
Radishes with their leaves
Tenderstem broccoli, mangetout, young peas in the pod or green beans, lightly blanched and cooled
Chicory, pea shoots and/or little gem leaves
Cherry tomatoes on the vine

1 Place the feta, lemon zest and juice, olive oil, yogurt, herbs and rocket in a blender or food processor. Blend until smooth and creamy. Taste and season with a little salt and plenty of pepper; remember the feta is already salty, so you may not need much.

2 Spoon the dip into a serving bowl and smooth the top. Scatter over the finely chopped nuts and seeds for texture and drizzle with oil.

3 Arrange the crudités on a large platter or board around the dip, grouping the different vegetables together for colour and contrast. Serve straight away, letting everyone help themselves by dipping and scooping.

SUPER-FUN PRAWN COCKTAILS

MAKES 12–16 SHOT GLASSES, DEPENDING ON SIZE

I love lining these up on a big tray – soft pink prawns, pale green avocado and crisp lettuce showing through the glass – then finishing each with a tiny mint leaf or a sliver of spring onion so they look really fresh. They're perfect passed around with a glass of something cold in hand, or cluster them in the middle of a table so guests can help themselves. For making ahead, you can shred the lettuce, slice the spring onions and mix the cocktail sauce several hours in advance, keeping everything chilled in separate containers. The prawns can be cooked (or simply seasoned if using ready-cooked) earlier in the day and stored in the refrigerator, well covered. Just assemble close to serving time so the lettuce stays crisp and the avocado doesn't discolour; if you need to prep the avocado a little ahead, toss it gently with lemon juice to help keep it green. Yum, let's party!

300g (10½oz) raw or cooked peeled prawns, or langoustines, if you can get them
1 cos lettuce, shredded
4 spring onions, thinly sliced, plus more (optional) to serve
2 ripe avocados, pitted and peeled, thinly sliced or chopped, plus more (optional) to serve
Sea salt and freshly ground black pepper

For the cocktail sauce
6 tablespoons mayonnaise
4 tablespoons tomato ketchup
1 teaspoon cayenne pepper, or to taste
Juice of 1 lemon, or to taste
1 tablespoon finely chopped mint leaves, plus more (optional) to serve

1. Cook the prawns, if they are raw, in salted boiling water (see page 176). Leave to cool.
2. In a bowl, toss the shredded lettuce with the sliced spring onions and a little seasoning.
3. For the cocktail sauce, mix the mayonnaise, ketchup, cayenne, lemon juice and chopped mint in a small bowl. Season to taste, adding more cayenne or lemon if you like it punchier.
4. To assemble, place a small forkful of the lettuce mixture in the base of each shot glass. Add a few pieces of avocado, then 3–4 prawns per glass, or more, depending on size. Spoon a little cocktail sauce over the top of each.
5. Chill until ready to serve, then finish with an extra grind of pepper and mint leaves, avocado slices or spring onion slices on top.

THE BEST BURGERS

SERVES 4

I love turning burgers into an occasion, unveiling a platter of juicy patties, toasted buns and lots of bowls of toppings so everyone can build their own. Keep them full-sized for a generous, two-handed burger, or shape the mixture into smaller patties for bite-sized party burgers that people can eat standing up with a drink in hand. Set everything out on a big board on the table and let guests stack theirs exactly how they like them. Feel free to scale the recipe up, for a bigger crowd.

For the burgers

½ tablespoon unsalted butter
1 tablespoon olive oil, plus more to cook
½ small onion, very finely chopped
1 garlic clove, finely grated or crushed
1 teaspoon chopped thyme leaves
500g (1lb 2oz) good-quality minced steak, ideally 15–20 per cent fat
1 teaspoon Dijon mustard
1 teaspoon Worcestershire sauce
1 egg yolk
1 tablespoon mayonnaise
30g (1oz) fresh breadcrumbs
Sea salt and freshly ground black pepper

To serve

4 slices of Emmental or Gruyère
4 brioche burger buns, halved
4 heaped tablespoons mayonnaise
3 teaspoons Dijon mustard
1 little gem lettuce, leaves separated
Handful of sliced gherkins
2 ripe tomatoes, thickly sliced

1 Melt the butter with the 1 tablespoon of olive oil in a frying pan over a medium-low heat. Add the onion, garlic and thyme with a pinch of salt and sauté gently for about 5 minutes, until the onion is soft and lightly golden. Transfer to a plate and leave to cool slightly.

2 In a bowl, combine the minced steak, mustard, Worcestershire sauce, egg yolk, mayo, breadcrumbs and the cooled onion mixture. Season generously with salt and pepper. Using clean hands, mix until everything is evenly combined, but avoid overworking the meat. Divide into 4 equal portions. Shape each into a ball, then flatten into patties slightly wider than your buns (they shrink as they cook). Use your thumb to press a small indent in the centres to help them cook evenly. Chill for 20–30 minutes, to help them hold their shape.

3 Heat a drizzle of olive oil on the hotplate of a barbecue, or in a large nonstick frying pan or griddle over a medium-high heat on the hob. Add the burgers and cook for 4–5 minutes on each side for medium, or to your liking, turning only once.

4 Transfer the burgers to a baking tray and top each with a slice of cheese. Pop under a hot grill (or cover with a barbecue lid or cloche) for 1–2 minutes, until the cheese is melted and bubbling. At the same time, lightly toast the cut sides of the brioche buns.

5 In a small bowl, mix the mayonnaise and Dijon mustard, then spread over the inside of the buns. Layer the bases with lettuce, add the cheesey burgers and finish with sliced gherkins and tomatoes. Top with the brioche lids and serve straight away.

TUSCAN BARBECUE CHICKEN

SERVES 8

All the work here happens in advance, and by the time everyone arrives, the garden smells of wood smoke, lemon and garlic. Mix the marinade and coat the chicken the day before, then leave it in the refrigerator so the flavours develop. When it's time to cook, you can just focus on the chicken and enjoy your guests.

4 tablespoons olive oil, plus more for brushing
Finely grated zest and juice of 2 lemons, plus lemon wedges to serve
6 garlic cloves, finely grated or crushed
3 tablespoons finely chopped rosemary leaves, plus more to serve
1 tablespoon thyme leaves (optional but lovely)
1 teaspoon dried oregano
150g (5½oz) mixed olives (green and/or black), pitted and roughly chopped
1 teaspoon sea salt, plus more to taste
½ teaspoon freshly ground black pepper
½ teaspoon chilli flakes (optional)
4 large skin-on chicken legs, separated into thighs and drumsticks to give 8 pieces
4 skin-on, bone-in chicken breasts (the bone-in part is optional, but adds flavour)

1 In a bowl, mix the olive oil, lemon zest and juice, garlic, rosemary, thyme, if using, oregano, chopped olives, salt, pepper and chilli flakes, if using. Stir well to make a loose, fragrant marinade.

2 Place the chicken in a bowl, pour the marinade over and turn everything so it is well coated, getting some of the olives and herbs tucked under the skin where you can. Cover and chill for at least 2 hours, ideally overnight. Bring to room temperature for 30 minutes before cooking.

3 Heat the barbecue, or if using an oven, preheat it to 200°C fan (425°F), Gas Mark 7 and line a large roasting tray with baking parchment or foil.

4 To barbecue the chicken, brush the grates with oil. Shake off and reserve excess marinade and place the chicken skin-side down over the hotter side of the barbecue. Sear for 3–4 minutes until nicely golden and lightly charred. Turn and sear the other side for another 3–4 minutes. Move the chicken to the cooler side of the barbecue, close the lid and cook for 25–35 minutes, turning occasionally and brushing with the reserved marinade, until cooked through and the juices run clear (if you have a probe thermometer, the internal temperature should be about 75°C / 167°F at the thickest part). Boil the reserved marinade separately in a saucepan until thickened and syrupy.

5 If going the oven route, arrange the chicken on a baking tray, spoon over all the marinade and roast for 35-40 minutes, turning once, until golden and cooked through. You can finish with 3-5 minutes under a hot grill for extra char.

6 Transfer the chicken to a warmed platter, spoon over any juices and olives from the roasting tray or saucepan and rest for 5–10 minutes. Scatter with a little chopped rosemary and serve with lemon wedges for squeezing over.

STICKY HARISSA HONEY RIBS

SERVES 6

Sticky, sweet and just the right amount of spicy, these ribs are the sort of thing that makes everyone go quiet for a moment when they take the first bite. The meat is cooked low and slow until it's almost falling off the bone, then blasted at a high heat with a glossy harissa, honey and whiskey glaze so it turns dark, caramelized and gloriously sticky. They're perfect for a summer party, finished on the barbecue and eaten with fingers and a stack of napkins, but just as good in the colder months cooked entirely in the oven and piled up in the middle of the table. However you serve them, they're the kind of crowd-pleasing dish that people remember.

2kg (4lb 8oz) pork belly rib racks, in 2–3 large racks

For the marinade

150g (5½oz) clear honey
150ml (5fl oz) sweet soy sauce (kecap manis)
150ml (5fl oz) whiskey
2–3 tablespoons harissa paste
4cm (1½-inch) piece of root ginger, peeled and finely grated
1 teaspoon toasted sesame oil
½ teaspoon ground cinnamon

1. In a bowl or jug, whisk together the honey, sweet soy, whiskey, harissa, grated ginger, sesame oil and cinnamon to make the marinade. Place the rib racks in a large roasting tin or deep baking tray in a single layer. Pour the marinade over, turning the ribs so they are well coated. Cover loosely and refrigerate for at least 4 hours, or overnight if you can.
2. When ready to cook, heat the oven to 120°C fan (275°F), Gas Mark 1. Remove the ribs from the refrigerator and let them sit at room temperature for 20–30 minutes. Lift them out of the marinade, letting excess drip back into the tray, and pour the remaining marinade into a bowl. Set the ribs back in the roasting tin, meaty-side up, and cover tightly with foil.
3. Roast for 3½–4 hours, until the meat is very tender and almost falling off the bone, basting once or twice during cooking with some of the reserved marinade, or the juices from the tin.
4. Towards the end of the cooking time, pour the reserved marinade into a small saucepan. Bring to the boil, then reduce the heat and simmer for 10–15 minutes, until thickened and syrupy.
5. When the ribs are tender, remove the foil and carefully cut between the bones. Increase the oven temperature to 200°C fan (425°F), Gas Mark 7, or heat a barbecue to high.
6. Brush the ribs generously with the reduced marinade and return them to the hot oven (or barbecue) for about 10 minutes. Turn, brush again with more marinade, and cook for a further 5–7 minutes, until sticky, dark and caramelized around the edges. Pile on to a warmed platter and serve straight away, with napkins at the ready.

CHARRED CORN ON THE COB with lime, chilli & Parmesan

SERVES 8

Corn is one of my favourite vegetables to grow in the garden. When I move the seedlings out from the glasshouse, they always look so fragile, as if they'll never survive, but once they push through and grow past about 15cm (6 inches) tall, they suddenly take off, turning into these towering green structures in the beds. There is simply nothing like that first grilled corn on the cob of the year, eaten outside, with tons of salted butter and black pepper. This version keeps all that sweetness and smokiness, but adds a bright mix of lime and chilli. The lime cuts through the richness and makes everything taste fresher, while the gentle heat from the chilli and the salty Parmesan cling to the kernels, giving each bite a hot, sharp, savoury edge that's completely addictive.

8 corn on the cob, husks removed or pulled inside-out away from the cob and tied together
2 tablespoons olive oil, or melted unsalted butter
60g (2¼oz) unsalted butter, softened
Finely grated zest and juice of 2 limes, plus lime wedges to serve
1–2 teaspoons chilli flakes, or chilli powder
60–80g (2¼–2¾oz) finely grated Parmesan
Small handful of coriander or parsley leaves, finely chopped (optional)
Sea salt and freshly ground black pepper

1. Bring a very large pan of salted water to the boil. Add the corn and simmer for 5–6 minutes until just tender, then drain well. Pat dry with kitchen paper and brush lightly with the oil or butter.
2. Heat a griddle pan or barbecue to high. Char the corn for 8–10 minutes, turning regularly, until lightly blackened in spots and smelling smoky. If you have left the husks on, make sure they are kept away from the flames.
3. Meanwhile, in a small bowl, mix the softened butter with the lime zest, 1 tablespoon of lime juice, chilli flakes or powder to taste, a pinch of salt and a good grind of pepper.
4. While the corn is still hot, brush or spoon the lime-chilli butter generously over all sides. Sprinkle immediately with the grated Parmesan so it clings to the warm corn, then scatter over the chopped herbs, if using.
5. Pile on to a platter and serve at once, with lime wedges for squeezing over.

THREE BEAN SALAD with Corn, Peppers & Lime

SERVES 8

Beans are one of my go-to ways to feed a crowd; they're delicious, inexpensive and so good for you, packed with fibre and plant protein. Here, they're tossed with sweet, fresh corn cut straight from the cob, crunchy red peppers and a sharp lime and chilli dressing, so every mouthful is bright and satisfying. It's the perfect make-ahead salad for a big garden party: it only improves as it sits, and it brings a big bowl of colour and health to the table for very little effort.

3 corn on the cob, husks removed
400g (14oz) can of black beans, drained and rinsed
400g (14oz) can of kidney beans, drained and rinsed
400g (14oz) can of cannellini beans, drained and rinsed
2 red peppers, deseeded and chopped
1 small red onion, finely chopped

For the lime dressing
120ml (4fl oz) olive oil
80ml (2¾fl oz) red wine vinegar
Finely grated zest and juice of 3–4 limes, or to taste
2 teaspoons chilli flakes, or to taste
3 tablespoons chopped coriander or parsley leaves
Sea salt and freshly ground black pepper

1. Hold each corn cob upright on a chopping board and carefully slice down the sides with a sharp knife to remove the kernels. Tip them into a dry frying pan and toast over a medium–high heat for 3–4 minutes, stirring often, until just tender and lightly charred in places. Set aside to cool.
2. For the dressing, whisk together the olive oil, red wine vinegar, lime zest and juice, chilli flakes and a generous pinch each of salt and pepper until emulsified. Stir in the chopped coriander or parsley. Taste and adjust the balance: you want it bright, citrusy and with a gentle heat.
3. In a large bowl, combine all the beans, the red peppers, cooled corn kernels and red onion. Pour the dressing over the salad and toss everything together until well coated. Taste and adjust the seasoning, adding more lime, salt or chilli if you like.
4. Leave to stand for at least 20–30 minutes before serving, so the beans have time to soak up the flavours. Serve at room temperature.

SUMMER POTATO SALAD with Peas & Radishes

SERVES 4

I love growing radishes, because they reward you so quickly, and in this recipe, their peppery crunch is the perfect contrast to soft, warm potatoes. The peas bring a natural sweetness and a pop of green that always makes this platter look generous and hopeful. Tossed together in a bright lemon vinaigrette, with herbs you've snipped on your way back into the kitchen, this feels simple, colourful and absolutely made for passing around a long, happy table outside. Make double the recipe for a big party.

900g (2lb) baby potatoes (new potatoes or Jersey Royals)
3 tablespoons finely chopped mixed herbs (mint, chives or parsley), plus 1 tablespoon torn mint leaves, plus more to serve
2 tablespoons olive oil, plus more if needed
2 shallots, finely chopped
Finely grated zest and juice of 1 lemon, plus more lemon juice if needed
1 teaspoon Dijon mustard, or to taste
100g (3½oz) fresh or frozen peas
10 radishes, finely sliced
Sea salt and freshly ground black pepper

1. Place the potatoes in a saucepan and cover with cold water. Add the 1 tablespoon of torn mint leaves and a generous pinch of salt. Put the lid on, bring to the boil over a high heat, then reduce to a simmer and cook for 15–20 minutes, or until just tender when pierced with the tip of a knife.
2. Meanwhile, warm a small frying pan over a medium heat. Add the olive oil, followed by the shallots and a pinch of salt. Cook for 3–4 minutes, until soft and translucent but not coloured. Tip into a large bowl and leave to cool slightly.
3. Whisk the lemon zest and juice and Dijon mustard into the warm shallots, seasoning well with salt and pepper. Taste and adjust: you want a bright, lemony dressing with a gentle mustard heat.
4. If using fresh peas, blanch them in lightly salted boiling water for 1–2 minutes, then drain and refresh briefly under cold water to keep their colour. If using frozen peas, cook them in boiling salted water for 2–3 minutes, then drain and refresh in the same way. Drain very well.
5. Drain the potatoes well and leave for a minute to steam-dry, then slice them in half while still warm and add them straight to the bowl with the lemon dressing. Gently toss so the warm potatoes absorb the flavours.
6. Add the peas, sliced radishes and chopped mixed herbs and toss again, being careful not to break up the potatoes. Taste and adjust the seasoning, adding a final squeeze of lemon juice or a drizzle more olive oil if needed. Serve slightly warm or at room temperature, with a few more herbs scattered over the top.

CRUNCHY APPLE SLAW

SERVES 6

The kind of slaw I always want on the table at a big summer gathering: crisp, cold and full of crunch to sit alongside all the slower, softer dishes. It's sharp and creamy at the same time, with sweet red apples, peppery cabbage and the clean, aromatic crunch of celery, all wrapped up in a lemony horseradish dressing that wakes everything up. It cuts beautifully through rich barbecued meats and roasted vegetables, and it keeps well in the refrigerator, so you can make it ahead of time and leave it to let the flavours get to know each other. A few years ago, I started growing celery from seed, and now I can't imagine being without it in the garden. I bring the seeds on slowly in the greenhouse; they take a good couple of months to become sturdy little seedlings, but once they're established and I move them out into the beds, they absolutely take off. From then on, I have celery for the whole summer and well into early autumn, and its flavour is so much brighter and sweeter than anything I can buy. Tossing that home-grown celery through this slaw, knowing it has come all the way from seed to bowl in my own garden, makes it feel even more special and completely worth the patience it takes.

100g (3½oz) mayonnaise
2 teaspoons finely chopped flat leaf parsley leaves
Finely grated zest and juice of 1 lemon, or 1 large lime
½ teaspoon sea salt, plus more to taste
50g (1¾oz) freshly grated horseradish, or ready-prepared horseradish, or to taste
¼ red cabbage, core removed, finely shredded
4 celery sticks (200–250g / 7–9oz), peeled, halved lengthways and thinly sliced
4 crisp red eating apples, cored and cut into matchsticks
1 carrot, cut into matchsticks
Freshly ground black pepper

1 In a large bowl, whisk together the mayonnaise, parsley, lemon zest and juice, salt, a good grind of black pepper and the horseradish. Taste and adjust the seasoning: you want a creamy, bright dressing with a gentle heat from the horseradish.

2 Add the shredded red cabbage, celery, apples and carrot to the bowl. Toss everything together until the vegetables are well coated in the dressing.

3 Cover and leave to marinate in the refrigerator for about 1 hour before serving, to let the flavours mingle and the cabbage soften slightly while staying crunchy. Toss again and check the seasoning just before you take it to the table.

CARROT, RAISIN & ALMOND SALAD with Mint & Coriander

SERVES 6

One of those salads that can happily sit in the middle of the table and go with almost everything. It's all about texture and brightness: the crunch of nuts and celery, the chew of raisins and a lemony honey dressing that feels light but still satisfying. The herbs make it sing: cool mint and fresh coriander thread their way through every forkful, giving the salad a sunny, almost Moroccan feel that works beautifully alongside grilled meats, fish or a spread of summer salads. I love making this when sweet summer carrots are at their best, pulled straight from the garden and still warm from the sun. Their natural sweetness means you don't need much honey in the dressing, and they hold their crunch even after sitting in the bowl for a while, so this is perfect for feeding a crowd.

80g (2¾oz) raisins
5 carrots, coarsely grated
2 celery sticks, thinly sliced
1 tablespoon finely chopped mint leaves
1 tablespoon finely chopped coriander
50g (1¾oz) whole almonds, roughly chopped

For the dressing
100ml (3½fl oz) extra virgin olive oil
Juice of 1 lemon, or to taste
1 teaspoon Dijon mustard
2 teaspoons clear honey
Sea salt and freshly ground black pepper

1. In a small bowl or jar, whisk together the olive oil, lemon juice, Dijon mustard, honey, a pinch of salt and a good grind of pepper until emulsified. Add the raisins to the dressing and leave to soak for about 5 minutes so they plump up.
2. Place the grated carrots in a large bowl. Add the celery, mint, coriander and almonds, then pour over the raisins and all the dressing. Toss everything together until well coated, then taste and adjust the seasoning, adding a little more lemon, salt or pepper if needed.
3. Serve straight away, or let it sit for 10–15 minutes to allow the flavours to mingle.

LEMON JELLY

SERVES 10–12 (FOR A 1.5–2-LITRE / 2½–3½-PINT JELLY MOULD)

A wonderfully old-fashioned pudding that never fails to delight. There's something so decadent and theatrical about turning out a beautiful jelly from its mould, shimmering and softly wobbling, yet it's also incredibly refreshing. It's a real crowd-pleaser, because it looks so special, and can handily be made a day ahead, leaving you free to simply unmould it and bring it to the table. Serve it with lemon ice cream, if you can, as the smooth creamy ice cream and sharp, clear jelly is such a lovely pairing: cool, elegant and full of sunshine. Nostalgic in the very best way, a little bit grand, a little bit playful and guaranteed to make everyone happy!

12 gelatine leaves, or follow the packet instructions to set 1.5–2 litres (2½–3½ pints) liquid
300g (10½oz) caster sugar, plus more if needed
300ml (10fl oz) freshly squeezed lemon juice (10–12 lemons), plus the finely grated zest of 4 lemons, plus more lemon zest to serve
1 teaspoon vanilla extract (optional, but lovely and softens the sharpness)

To serve (optional)
Lemon ice cream
Mint leaves

1. Place the gelatine leaves in a bowl of cold water and leave to soften for 10 minutes. Pour 500ml (18fl oz) of water into a saucepan and add the sugar and lemon zest. Heat gently, stirring, until the sugar has dissolved, then bring just up to a simmer. Take off the heat and leave for 10 minutes so the zest infuses.
2. Squeeze the softened gelatine to remove excess water. Stir it into the hot (not boiling) lemon-sugar mixture until completely dissolved. Stir in the lemon juice and the vanilla, if using. Taste and adjust the sweetness: remember the jelly will be slightly less sweet and a little sharper once chilled and set, but this should be bright and refreshing, not too sour.
3. Lightly rinse your jelly mould with very cold water (or briefly chill it in the refrigerator) to help with release later. Strain the lemon mixture through a fine sieve into a large jug to remove the zest and any bits. Pour gently into the mould, let it cool to room temperature, then cover and chill for at least 6 hours, preferably overnight, until completely set.
4. To turn out, briefly dip the mould in a bowl of hot (not boiling) water for a few seconds, being careful not to let water spill into the jelly. Place a cold serving plate on top, invert and give a gentle shake until the jelly releases.
5. Serve with lemon ice cream if you like, scattered with more lemon zest and mint leaves.

Menu

Harvest Supper

Curried Parsnip
& Apple Soup
with Crispy Bacon
& Apple Matchsticks

Chocolate Beef Chilli

Orchard Tarte Tatin

CURRIED PARSNIP & APPLE SOUP with crispy bacon & apple matchsticks

SERVES 6–8

I love serving this in tea cups; such a simple thing to do, it makes the soup a real 'event', as impressive to look at as it's easy to cook.

80g (2¾oz) salted butter
6 large parsnips, peeled and chopped
2 garlic cloves, finely grated or crushed
2 onions, chopped
2 potatoes, peeled and chopped
2 cooking apples, peeled, cored and chopped
1 tablespoon plain flour
1 tablespoon medium curry powder
2 litres (3½ pints) hot vegetable stock (for homemade, see page 125)
200ml (7fl oz) double cream
Sea salt and freshly ground black pepper

To serve

100g (3½oz) pancetta or smoked streaky bacon lardons
1 eating apple
Juice of ½ lemon
2 tablespoons finely chopped coriander

1 Melt the butter in a saucepan over a low heat. Once the butter has melted, stir in the parsnips, garlic, onions, potatoes and cooking apples and season with salt and pepper. Cover and cook for 10 minutes, stirring occasionally, until the parsnips and apples are tender.

2 Remove the lid and stir in the flour and curry powder to coat all the ingredients evenly. Pour in the hot stock, stirring well, then bring to the boil. Reduce the heat and simmer for another 10 minutes.

3 Pour the soup into a blender and blend until smooth, then add the cream and blend for a final 10 seconds. Pour back into the saucepan and gently warm through (the cream will have brought the temperature of the soup down). You can also blend this with a stick blender.

4 Meanwhile, sauté the pancetta or smoked streaky bacon in a dry frying pan until crisp, then remove to a plate lined with kitchen paper.

5 Cut the eating apple into thin matchsticks and toss them in a bowl with the lemon juice, to stop them from discolouring.

6 To serve, pour the soup into warmed bowls and scatter with the apple matchsticks, crispy pancetta or bacon, or coriander. I like all three!

CHOCOLATE BEEF CHILLI

SERVES 6

Don't worry, this doesn't taste 'chocolatey'! It's exactly the kind of dish I like to make a day ahead, because time improves it. During a night in the refrigerator, the spices soften, the tomatoes mellow and all the flavours have a chance to marry, so the next day it tastes deeper and more harmonious. I serve it with rice and lots of garnishes on the table – sour cream, sharp Cheddar, fresh jalapeños, coriander and lime wedges – so everyone can build their perfect bowl.

2 tablespoons olive oil
300g (10½oz) minced beef
1 small onion, finely chopped
3cm (1¼-inch) piece of root ginger, peeled and grated
3 garlic cloves, crushed
1 teaspoon ground cumin
1 teaspoon ground cinnamon
1 teaspoon chilli flakes
100g (3½oz) pancetta, cubed
100g (3½oz) chorizo, cut into small pieces
400g (14oz) can of cherry or chopped tomatoes
1 tablespoon light brown sugar
2 teaspoons dried oregano
2 bay leaves
1 tablespoon tomato ketchup
2 corn on the cob, husks removed
50g (1¾oz) 70 per cent cocoa solids chocolate, finely chopped or grated
400g (14oz) can of kidney beans, drained and rinsed
Sea salt and freshly ground black pepper

To serve
Basmati rice
4 fresh jalapeños, sliced
150–200g (5½–7oz) mature Cheddar, grated
300g (10½oz) sour cream
Coriander leaves
Lime wedges (optional but lovely)

1 Place a large flameproof casserole over a medium-high heat. Add 1 tablespoon of the olive oil, then the minced beef. Cook, breaking it up with a wooden spoon, until well browned all over. Season lightly with salt and pepper. Transfer the browned meat to a plate and set aside.

2 Add the remaining oil to the same dish. Stir in the onion, ginger and garlic with a pinch of salt, and cook for 3–4 minutes over a medium heat until softened and fragrant. Stir in the cumin, cinnamon and chilli flakes and cook for another minute so the spices become aromatic.

3 Add the pancetta and chorizo and cook for 3–4 minutes until they start to release their fat and take on a little colour. Return the browned minced beef and stir well. Pour in the tomatoes along with 300ml (½ pint) of water, then add the brown sugar, dried oregano, bay leaves and tomato ketchup. Season with salt and pepper and stir. Bring to the boil, then reduce the heat to low, cover with a lid and simmer very gently for 90 minutes, stirring occasionally, until thick and rich.

4 Preheat the oven to 180°C fan (400°F), Gas Mark 6. Put the corn cobs on a baking tray and roast for 20 minutes, turning once, until tender and lightly golden in spots. Set aside to cool slightly.

5 Stir the chocolate and beans into the chilli and simmer uncovered for 20 minutes, until glossy and slightly thickened. Taste and adjust the seasoning. Using a sharp knife, slice the roasted corn kernels off the cobs and stir them through the chilli. Serve with bowls of rice, sliced jalapeños, grated Cheddar, sour cream, coriander and lime wedges, if you like.

ORCHARD TARTE TATIN

SERVES 6

My most-requested dessert recipe of all time. It looks gloriously impressive when you turn it out, but it's actually very simple once you understand two key tarte Tatin rules. First, let the caramel get properly rich and deep in colour before you add the fruit; second, always use a good all-butter pastry, because the flavour and flaky texture make all the difference. When you flip it out and bring it to the table with a bowl of cold crème fraîche, there's always a little hush. Once you've mastered the method, try swapping the apples for firm-but-ripe pears, just-ripe plums, or firm apricots.

165g (5¾oz) caster sugar
65g (2½oz) salted butter, chopped
5 Gala apples, peeled, cored and quartered
Plain flour, to dust
1 ready-rolled all-butter puff pastry sheet, chilled
Crème fraîche, to serve

1 Place a 20cm (8-inch) cast-iron pan or ovenproof frying pan over a low heat. Add the caster sugar and 100ml (3½fl oz) of water and stir until the sugar has dissolved. Once dissolved, stop stirring and increase the heat to medium-high. Let the syrup bubble for 10–14 minutes, swirling the pan occasionally, until it turns a rich amber. Be patient: a pale caramel will give a flat, sweet tart, whereas a deep golden-brown brings that proper, grown-up bittersweet flavour you want.

2 As soon as the caramel is a deep golden amber, take the pan off the heat and carefully whisk or stir in the chopped butter until smooth.

3 Preheat the oven to 180°C fan (400°F), Gas Mark 6.

4 Arrange the apple quarters in the hot caramel with the cut sides facing up, packing them in tightly and slightly overlapping so they completely cover the base; they will shrink a little as they cook, so it's better to squeeze them in. Set the pan back over a low heat for 5–10 minutes so the apples start to soften in the caramel.

5 On a lightly floured work surface, roll out the puff pastry so it's slightly larger than the pan, 23–26cm (9–10½ inches) in diameter. Cut out a neat circle. Lay the pastry over the apples, tucking the edges down around the inside of the pan so the fruit is snugly enclosed, like tucking in a blanket. Use a sharp knife to make 3 small slits in the centre to allow steam to escape.

6 Place the pan in the preheated oven and bake for 35–45 minutes, until the pastry is puffed, crisp and deep golden. Remove from the oven and allow the tart to sit for 5–10 minutes to let the bubbling caramel settle.

7 To turn out, place a large heatproof serving plate over the pan, hold it firmly with oven gloves and carefully invert in one confident movement so the tart drops on to the plate. Lift off the pan: the apples should now be sitting proudly on top in their glossy caramel. Serve warm in generous slices with a cool dollop of crème fraîche.

Menu

Winter Pub Dinner at The Cork Arms

Roast Pumpkin,
Burrata & Chilli

Chicken Fricassée

Pistachio Tiramisu

ROAST PUMPKIN, BURRATA & CHILLI

SERVES 6

Pumpkins deserve a dish as beautiful to look at as they are to grow, and I think this is it. In late summer and early autumn, ours hang down over the archways in the walled garden, like lanterns suspended in mid-air… it's the most magical sight. I especially love the Crown Prince variety: that soft silver skin giving way to the richest, deepest orange flesh. Roasted until caramelized at the edges, it's sweet and nutty, and makes the perfect base for cool, silky burrata and a scattering of fiery chilli. The contrast of textures and temperatures – hot sweet nutty pumpkin, silky-cool and creamy cheese, the sharp prickle of heat and a little balsamic – means this feels both comforting and a little bit glamorous, even restaurant-worthy, and definitely makes every mouthful feel special. You can make it with butternut squash too, but if you can get your hands on a beautiful eating pumpkin, it really sings. This is such a great party starter because it looks so impressive, yet is incredibly simple to put together. The pumpkin does most of the work for you: once it's sliced and in the oven, it roasts away happily while you get on with everything else.

1.2–1.5kg (2lb 12oz–3lb 5oz) pumpkin or butternut squash
4–5 tablespoons extra virgin olive oil, plus more to serve
3 balls of burrata (150–200g / 5½–7oz each)
2 red chillies, finely sliced, deseeded or not, to taste
2–3 tablespoons good balsamic vinegar
Sea salt and freshly ground black pepper

1. Preheat the oven to 180°C fan (400°F), Gas Mark 6.
2. Cut the pumpkin into 2–3cm- (1-inch-) thick wedges, removing the seeds. If the skin is very tough, peel it; but if it's a tender eating pumpkin or butternut squash, you can leave the skin on. Spread the wedges over 2 baking trays so they lie in a single layer.
3. Drizzle with the olive oil, season generously with salt and pepper and toss to coat. Roast for 25–35 minutes, turning once, until the pumpkin is tender and caramelized at the edges.
4. Arrange the hot roasted pumpkin on a large warmed platter. Tear the burrata into pieces and nestle them over the pumpkin so they just start to soften in the warmth.
5. Scatter over the finely chopped chillies. Season again with a little more salt and pepper, then finish with a good drizzle of extra virgin olive oil and the balsamic vinegar.
6. Serve straight away, with plenty of crusty bread or focaccia for mopping up the juices.

CHICKEN FRICASSÉE

SERVES 6

A fabulous French classic that feels far more luxurious than you'd think from the effort it takes. It's everything you want from comfort cooking: tender chicken in a silky sauce, a little cream, bright tarragon and a squeeze of lemon juice to lift it all. It's elegant in that very French way, rich but not heavy, comforting but refined enough to bring to the table for guests. The flavours only improve if you cook it ahead and let it rest: it reheats beautifully. Herby rice works wonderfully alongside.

75g (2¾oz) unsalted butter
1½ tablespoons olive oil
12 skin-on, bone-in chicken thighs
1½ onions, finely chopped
1½ carrots, finely chopped
1½ celery sticks, finely chopped
330g (11½oz) mushrooms, quartered
3 garlic cloves, finely grated or crushed
1½ tablespoons plain flour
300ml (½ pint) dry white wine
1.5 litres (2½ pints) chicken stock
3 flat leaf parsley sprigs
2 small thyme sprigs
1–2 bay leaves
90ml (6 tablespoons) double cream
3 tablespoons finely chopped tarragon leaves
Juice of 1–1½ lemons, or to taste
Sea salt and freshly ground black pepper

1. Place a wide flameproof casserole over a medium heat and add the butter and olive oil. Season the chicken well with salt and pepper, then add it to the pan skin-side down in a single layer. (You may need to do this in batches, depending on the size of your pan.) Cook for 8–10 minutes, turning once, until the skin is deep golden and the meat is well browned. Transfer the chicken to a plate and set aside.
2. Reduce the heat to medium-low. Add the onions, carrots and celery to the pan, scraping up any browned bits from the bottom with a wooden spoon. Season lightly, cover and cook for 8–10 minutes, stirring occasionally, until the vegetables are soft and lightly golden.
3. Remove the lid, add the mushrooms and garlic and stir to coat in the buttery juices. Cook uncovered for 5–7 minutes, until the mushrooms are golden and any moisture has evaporated. Season again with a little salt and pepper.
4. Sprinkle in the flour and stir well so it coats the vegetables. Cook for 1–2 minutes to cook out the raw flour taste. Return the chicken and any resting juices, pour in the wine, bring to the boil and let it bubble for 2–3 minutes to reduce slightly. Add the chicken stock and stir.
5. Tie the parsley sprigs, thyme and bay leaves together with kitchen twine to make a bouquet garni and add it to the pot. Bring everything up to a gentle boil, then reduce the heat to a low simmer. Cover and cook for 35–45 minutes, until the chicken is tender and cooked through and the sauce has reduced a little.
6. Remove the lid and discard the herb bundle. Stir in the cream, chopped tarragon and lemon juice, to taste. Simmer gently for a further 5 minutes, uncovered, to let the flavours come together. Taste and adjust the seasoning, adding more salt, pepper or lemon juice if needed.

PISTACHIO TIRAMISU

SERVES 6

I love this! It's a slightly glamorous make-ahead dessert for a small or large dinner party, as you can easily double up the recipe. You get all the silkiness of classic tiramisu, but with that gorgeous pistachio flavour running through the mascarpone cream and a good hit of coffee to keep it grown-up. The pistachio brings a gentle nuttiness and sweetness, espresso-soaked biscuits give you that familiar tiramisu bite and the cocoa and chopped nuts on top add just enough bitterness and crunch to balance everything out. It's the sort of pudding that tastes even better after a good chill in the refrigerator, which makes it perfect for entertaining; you can assemble it completely earlier in the day (or even the night before), then simply dust with cocoa and scatter with pistachios just before you bring it to the table. You will need six small individual trifle bowls or dessert glasses.

100ml (3½fl oz) strong espresso, cooled
18 boudoir biscuits (ladyfingers)
4 large egg yolks
120g (4½oz) caster sugar
115g (4oz) pistachio cream
500g (1lb 2oz) mascarpone
15g (½oz) cocoa powder
25g (1oz) pistachios, chopped

1. Arrange 6 small trifle bowls or dessert glasses on a tray or work surface. Put the coffee in a shallow dish. Briefly dip 9 boudoir biscuits briefly into the cold espresso (you want them soaked but not collapsing). Break the biscuits as necessary and divide them between the bowls, using 1½ biscuits in each bowl, to create a base layer.
2. To make the creamy mascarpone-pistachio mixture, place the egg yolks and caster sugar in a mixing bowl. Whisk together until very pale, thick and slightly increased in volume.
3. Add the pistachio cream and whisk again until fully combined. Then add the mascarpone and whisk slowly until the mixture is smooth, pale and just thick enough to hold soft peaks. Take care not to over-whisk, or it may become too loose.
4. Spoon or pipe half the pistachio mixture over the soaked biscuit bases. Briefly dip the remaining 9 boudoir biscuits in the espresso, then break them as needed and divide evenly between the bowls to form the second layer. Top each with the remaining pistachio mascarpone cream, smoothing the surface with the back of a spoon.
5. Cover and refrigerate for at least 4 hours, or ideally overnight, to allow the flavours to develop and the mixture to firm up. Just before serving, sift a thin layer of cocoa powder over and sprinkle with the finely chopped pistachios.

Menu

Christmas

STARTER

Chicken Liver Paté
with Brandy and Thyme

MAIN

Turkey with Parma Ham,
Orange & Thyme Butter

Golden Roasties
with Rosemary

Spiced Red Cabbage

Menu

Christmas

Snowy Sprouts
with Chestnuts

Christmas Turkey Gravy

Ruby Cranberry Sauce

DESSERTS

Jewel-Bright Berry
Christmas Trifles

Buttery Orange &
Brandy Mince Pies

CHICKEN LIVER PATÉ with brandy & thyme

SERVES 10

There are certain recipes that quietly become part of the rhythm of your life, and this paté is one of mine. I've been making it every Christmas for more than twenty-five years and it signals the start of the festivities. It's rich, silky and deeply comforting, perfect served as a light lunch or starter with crisp toast or brioche. For the festive season, I finish it with a layer of orange-scented clarified butter, scattered with dried cranberries and pistachios... it looks as beautiful as it tastes and feels wonderfully Christmassy!

2 tablespoons olive oil
350g (12oz) unsalted butter, softened
2 shallots, finely chopped
5 garlic cloves, finely grated or crushed
1kg (2lb 4oz) chicken livers, trimmed and cleaned
Pinch of freshly grated nutmeg (optional)
4 tablespoons brandy
2 tablespoons thyme leaves
Finely grated zest of 1 orange
Sea salt and freshly ground black pepper

For the topping
75g (2¾oz) unsalted butter
Finely grated zest of 1 orange
2 tablespoons finely chopped dried cranberries
2 tablespoons finely chopped pistachios

1 Heat the olive oil with a small knob of the butter in a large frying pan over a medium heat. Add the shallots and cook gently for 6–8 minutes until soft and translucent. Stir in the garlic and cook for another minute.

2 Increase the heat slightly and add the chicken livers. Cook for 8–10 minutes, turning occasionally, until browned on the outside but still slightly pink in the centre. Avoid overcooking. Season well with salt, pepper and nutmeg, if using.

3 Pour in the brandy and let it bubble for a minute, scraping up all the caramelized bits from the base of the pan. Add the thyme and orange zest, then remove from the heat.

4 Transfer to a food processor and blend until smooth. Allow to cool slightly, then gradually add the remaining softened butter, blending until fully incorporated and silky. Taste and adjust the seasoning. Spoon into a terrine lined with clingfilm, or serving dishes, and smooth the surface.

5 To make the clarified butter, gently melt the 75g (2¾oz) of butter in a small saucepan over a low heat. Skim off the white milk solids from the surface, then carefully pour the clear golden butter into a bowl, leaving any milky residue behind. Stir in the orange zest.

6 Pour the clarified butter over the paté. While still soft, scatter over the chopped cranberries and pistachios. Leave to set in the refrigerator for at least 3 hours, or ideally overnight.

7 Remove from the refrigerator 20 minutes before serving to allow the paté to soften slightly. Serve with toasted brioche or sourdough and a sharp cranberry or spiced fruit chutney.

BROADSPEAR

SPICED RED CABBAGE

SERVES 8

It simply doesn't feel like Christmas without this. Gently spiced, sweet and tangy, it fills the kitchen with the most comforting aroma as it cooks. I've made versions of it for years and it's one of my favourite sides to serve alongside roast meats, particularly turkey, goose, duck or ham. The beauty of red cabbage is that it only improves with time, making it perfect for preparing a day or two in advance, something every Christmas cook will appreciate. Leftovers are also delicious served at room temperature and I love it in a Boxing Day sandwich! A handful of dried cranberries or raisins stirred in towards the end adds a festive note, or a splash of Port gives extra richness.

25g (1oz) unsalted butter
1 tablespoon olive oil
1 onion, thinly sliced
800g (1lb 12oz) red cabbage, core removed and finely sliced
1 teaspoon ground cinnamon
½ teaspoon freshly grated nutmeg
4 cloves, lightly crushed, or ½ teaspoon ground cloves
2cm (¾-inch) piece of root ginger, peeled and finely grated
1 eating apple (about 200g / 7oz), peeled, cored and grated, plus 2 eating apples (about 300g / 10½oz), peeled, cored and sliced
100ml (3½fl oz) apple cider vinegar, plus more to taste
70g (2½oz) soft brown sugar, plus more to taste
Sea salt and freshly ground black pepper

1 Melt the butter with the olive oil in a large, heavy-based saucepan or flameproof casserole over a medium heat. Add the onion and cook gently for 5-6 minutes until soft and translucent.

2 Add the cabbage and toss well to coat in the butter. Cook for 5-8 minutes, stirring occasionally, until it begins to soften slightly. Season generously with salt and pepper.

3 Stir in the cinnamon, nutmeg, cloves and ginger, followed by the grated apple (not the sliced apples yet). Cook for a further 2-3 minutes to allow the spices to release their aroma.

4 Pour in the vinegar and sprinkle over the sugar. Stir well, then bring to a gentle simmer. Now arrange the sliced apples on top, cover with a lid and reduce the heat to low. Cook gently for 30-40 minutes, stirring occasionally, until the cabbage is tender but still retains a little texture. Avoid overcooking it; the cabbage should be tender but not mushy, with a slight bite.

5 Remove the lid for the final 10 minutes of cooking, to allow the liquid to reduce and the flavours to intensify. Taste and adjust the seasoning, balancing the sweetness and acidity with more sugar or vinegar if needed. Serve warm.

Clodagh's Cracking Cabbage

This is even better made 1–2 days in advance and reheated gently, as the flavour deepens beautifully. It freezes very well once completely cool; just reheat it slowly.

SNOWY SPROUTS with chestnuts

SERVES 6–8

Brussels sprouts are one of the real stars of my Christmas table, not just for their flavour but for the joy they bring in from the garden. I grow them myself, and cutting off the long stalk with all the sprouts attached is one of the most exciting moments on Christmas Eve... it feels like the true start of the celebrations! In the kitchen, I want to honour that excitement by cooking them in a way that feels generous and festive. Here, the sprouts stay bright and slightly crisp, while pancetta brings savoury richness, cranberries add little bursts of sharp-sweet flavour and chestnuts give a soft, nutty warmth. Marsala ties everything together with a gentle sweetness and gloss, so every forkful feels comforting and celebratory alongside the roast. A little orange zest or a squeeze of orange juice added with the Marsala works beautifully with the cranberries and chestnuts.

You can blanch the sprouts earlier in the day: cool them quickly in cold water, drain well, and keep in the refrigerator. Finish them in the pancetta pan just before serving. Aim for bright green sprouts with a slight bite; overcooking will dull both the colour and flavour.

1kg (2lb 4oz) Brussels sprouts
1 tablespoon olive oil
250g (9oz) pancetta, diced
50g (1¾oz) unsalted butter
100g (3½oz) fresh cranberries, or frozen and defrosted
250g (9oz) vacuum-packed chestnuts, roughly broken into large pieces
100ml (3½fl oz) Marsala
1 teaspoon chopped thyme leaves
2 teaspoons finely chopped flat leaf parsley leaves
Sea salt and freshly ground black pepper

1. Prepare the sprouts by trimming the bases and removing tired outer leaves. Cut any large sprouts in half, leaving small ones whole. Bring a large pan of salted water to the boil, add the sprouts and cook for 4–5 minutes until just tender but still with a little bite. Drain well and allow to steam-dry.
2. Heat the olive oil in a large frying pan over a medium-high heat. Add the pancetta and cook for 5–7 minutes until golden and crisp, releasing its fat.
3. Reduce the heat slightly, add the butter, cranberries and chestnuts and cook for 2–3 minutes until the cranberries begin to soften and the chestnuts are warmed and lightly caramelized in places. Pour in the Marsala and let it bubble for 1–2 minutes, scraping up any caramelized bits from the base of the pan so you capture all the flavour.
4. Add the drained sprouts to the pan and toss everything together over the heat for another 2–3 minutes so they're well coated and heated through. Stir in the thyme and parsley, then season generously with freshly ground black pepper. Taste and add a little salt if needed.
5. Transfer to a warmed serving dish, making sure the pancetta, cranberries and chestnuts are visible on top. Serve immediately.

TURKEY with Parma ham, orange & thyme butter

SERVES 8–10

My kind of Christmas turkey: succulent, fragrant and full of flavour at every layer. The orange and thyme butter keeps the meat beautifully moist and adds a gentle citrus brightness, and the Parma ham slowly crisps as it roasts, basting the bird and preventing it from drying out. It's a simple but transformative addition and one I now return to every year. The result is tender, juicy meat, deeply flavourful pan juices and that wonderful moment at the table when the crisp Parma ham is revealed.

The flavoured butter can be made up to three days in advance and kept chilled, plus the stuffing can be prepared the day before and stored in the refrigerator. You can stuff and butter the turkey and cover it with Parma ham early on Christmas morning, ready for roasting.

1 free-range turkey (4–4.5kg / 8lb 13oz–9lb 5oz)
2 bunches of thyme
1 orange, cut into wedges
10–12 slices of Parma ham
Sea salt and freshly ground black pepper

For the stuffing
80g (2¾oz) unsalted butter
2 onions, finely chopped
2 apples, peeled, cored and chopped
400g (14oz) good-quality pork sausagemeat
200g (7oz) fresh white breadcrumbs
1 tablespoon finely chopped thyme leaves
1 tablespoon chopped flat leaf parsley
½ teaspoon freshly grated nutmeg

For the butter
200g (7oz) salted butter, softened
2 tablespoons finely chopped thyme leaves
Finely grated zest of 2 oranges
1 tablespoon Dijon mustard

For the roasting tray
4 shallots, peeled and halved
3 carrots, cut into large chunks
1 garlic bulb, halved horizontally
4 small bunches of thyme
4 small bunches of sage

Turkey Cooking Times

3.5–5kg (8–12lb) Cook 3 hours 20 minutes–4 hours 40 minutes
5.5–6.5kg (12–14lb) Cook 4 hours 40 minutes–5 hours 20 minutes
6.5–8kg (14–18lb) Cook 5 hours 20 minutes–6 hours 40 minutes

1 Remove the turkey from the refrigerator 1 hour before cooking. Remove the giblets, pat the cavity dry and season well with salt and pepper. Stuff loosely with thyme and orange wedges. (The actual stuffing is yet to come!)

2 Make the stuffing. Melt the butter in a saucepan, add the onions and apples, cover and cook gently for 5 minutes until softened. Allow to cool, then mix in a bowl with the sausagemeat, breadcrumbs, herbs, nutmeg, salt and papper. Spoon some into the neck end of the turkey and a little into the cavity (do not overfill). Any extra can be baked separately in an ovenproof dish.

3 Mix all the butter ingredients together.

4 Preheat the oven to 180°C fan (400°F), Gas Mark 6. Gently loosen the skin over the breast and spread most of the butter underneath, being careful not to break the skin, then rub the remainder all over the outside of the bird. Lay the Parma ham slices over the breast, slightly overlapping so they form a protective layer. Tuck them neatly around the sides.

5 Arrange the shallots, carrots, garlic, thyme and sage in a large roasting tray and place the turkey on top. Roast for 45 minutes, then reduce the oven temperature to 160°C fan (350°F), Gas Mark 4. Baste the turkey, then cover loosely with foil and continue roasting, basting every 40–45 minutes. (See left for turkey-cooking timings.)

6 When there are 30–40 minutes before the end of cooking, remove the foil so the Parma ham can crisp and the turkey skin turn golden.

7 The turkey is cooked when the juices run clear from the thickest part of the thigh or a probe thermometer reads 75°C (167°F). Transfer to a serving platter, cover loosely with foil and rest for at least 30–45 minutes before carving.

GOLDEN ROASTIES with rosemary

SERVES 8

No Christmas table is complete without a bowl of golden, crispy roast potatoes, and I return to this recipe year after year. Fluffy within and wonderfully crisp on the outside, they're infused with rosemary, garlic and a hint of orange, which lifts and brightens the richness beautifully.

The extra step of gently crushing and pre-crisping the potatoes is what makes them truly special; it creates all those irresistible craggy edges that turn gloriously golden in the oven. If you're feeding a crowd, these can be prepared ahead, making Christmas Day that little bit more relaxed.

1.5kg (3lb 5oz) Maris Piper or King Edward potatoes, peeled
180g (6oz) goose fat
2 tablespoons finely chopped rosemary leaves, plus more to serve
Handful of garlic cloves
Zest of 1 orange, pared off in strips with a vegetable peeler, plus fine shavings of zest to serve
Sea salt and freshly ground black pepper

1. Preheat the oven to 200°C fan (425°F), Gas Mark 7. Place a large roasting tray in the oven to heat.
2. Cut the potatoes into even, large chunks. Place in a pan of cold salted water, bring to the boil, then reduce the heat and simmer for 10–12 minutes until just tender on the outside. Drain well, then return to the pan and gently shake or lightly crush with a masher to rough up the edges; this is key for achieving that crisp finish. Allow them to steam-dry for a few minutes.
3. Meanwhile, melt the goose fat in a large frying pan over a medium heat. Working in batches, add some of the potatoes and turn them gently until lightly golden and coated in the fat. Add a little of the rosemary, garlic and orange zest strips to each batch and cook for 30–60 seconds, just until fragrant, being careful not to let the garlic catch. Transfer to the hot roasting tray.
4. Once all the potatoes are in the tray with their goose fat, season generously with salt and pepper and roast for 30–40 minutes, turning once, until deeply golden and crisp. Transfer to a warmed serving dish and scatter with a little rosemary and a few fine shavings of fresh orange zest.

Clodagh's Stress-Free Roastie Tips

1. Add the potatoes to hot fat and a hot tray; they should instantly sizzle, as this helps form a crust.

2. Give the potatoes space in the tray, so they roast rather than steam.

3. Adding garlic during the pre-crisping step keeps it fragrant without burning in the oven.

4. You can parboil, rough up, and pre-crisp the potatoes up to 2–3 days ahead. Cool completely, then store covered in the refrigerator. Bring to room temperature, then continue from step 4, above.

CHRISTMAS TURKEY GRAVY

SERVES 8–10

This makes everything on the plate taste better. Made from the richly flavoured pan juices of the roast turkey, it's deep, savoury and full of character. The sweetness of the roasted vegetables and the herbs come together to create something truly special. I like to make it just before serving, using all those golden, caramelized bits from the roasting tray as they hold incredible flavour. If you're well prepared, you can also make it slightly ahead and gently reheat when needed.

Pan juices and roasted vegetables from the turkey tray
2 tablespoons plain flour
500–750ml (18fl oz–1¼ pints) hot, good-quality chicken or turkey stock
1 tablespoon redcurrant jelly (optional, for balance)
1 tablespoon Port or Madeira (optional)
Sea salt and freshly ground black pepper

1. Once the turkey is removed from the roasting tray, spoon off most of the excess fat, leaving behind about 2–3 tablespoons along with all the sticky, caramelized bits. Place the roasting tray over a medium heat on the hob (or transfer everything into a large saucepan if that's easier). Sprinkle in the flour and stir well, scraping up all the flavour from the base of the tray to form a roux. Cook for 1–2 minutes.
2. Gradually pour in the hot stock, whisking continuously to avoid lumps. Bring to a gentle simmer and cook for 5–10 minutes until the gravy thickens to your liking. Stir in the redcurrant jelly and Port or Madeira, if using, and allow them to melt into the gravy.
3. Strain through a sieve into a clean saucepan or jug, pressing down on the vegetables to extract all their flavour. Taste and adjust the seasoning with salt and pepper. Keep warm until ready to serve.

RUBY CRANBERRY SAUCE

SERVES 8

This vibrant, jewel-like sauce is one of those small but essential parts of the Christmas table. Warming ginger and sweet spice bring depth, while a whole chilli adds subtle, lingering heat. It's that balance – sweet, sour, warm and just a little fiery – that makes it so irresistible alongside rich roast meats such as turkey, goose or ham. I love how the cranberries burst as they cook, creating a naturally thick, glossy sauce. It's wonderfully simple to make and, even better, it can be prepared three or four days in advance and kept in the refrigerator, allowing the flavours to deepen and mellow. I recommend you double the recipe: it's so good in Boxing Day sandwiches, or served with paté or ham (see pages 248 and 196).

200g (7oz) caster sugar
2cm (¾-inch) piece of root ginger, peeled
5-6 cloves
1 cinnamon stick
1 red chilli, left whole and pricked once with a knife, or sliced open for more heat
400g (14oz) fresh cranberries
Finely grated zest of ½ orange (optional, but lovely)
Pinch of sea salt

1. Place the sugar and 100ml (3½fl oz) of water in a saucepan over a medium heat. Stir gently until the sugar has completely dissolved, then bring to a gentle simmer.
2. Stud the ginger with the cloves (this makes them easy to remove later), then add to the pan along with the cinnamon stick, chilli and cranberries. Simmer gently for 10–15 minutes, stirring occasionally, until the cranberries begin to burst and the sauce thickens slightly. If you prefer a smoother sauce, gently mash some of the cranberries as they cook.
3. Remove from the heat and stir in the orange zest, if using, and a small pinch of salt to enhance the flavour. Allow to cool slightly, then remove the ginger, cloves, cinnamon stick and chilli. The sauce will continue to thicken as it cools. Serve warm or at room temperature.

JEWEL-BRIGHT BERRY CHRISTMAS TRIFLES

SERVES 8

There's something wonderfully nostalgic about bringing trifles to the table at Christmas, and this version feels grown-up and indulgent. Finished with softly whipped cream and cherries on top, it's a dessert that looks spectacular for very little effort, and is ideal for making ahead so you can simply lift it from the refrigerator when everyone is ready for pudding.

500g (1lb 2oz) frozen mixed berries
70g (2½oz) golden caster sugar
50ml (1¾fl oz) crème de cassis
200g (7oz) shop-bought or homemade Madeira cake, cut into cubes or sliced
135g (4¾oz) pack of raspberry jelly
250g (9oz) mascarpone
1 tablespoon vanilla extract
500ml (18fl oz) good-quality thick custard, chilled (shop-bought or homemade)
300ml (10½fl oz) double cream, softly whipped
Handful of fresh cherries

1 Place the frozen berries and sugar in a saucepan over a low heat. Gently cook for 3–4 minutes until the berries start to soften and release their juices, then stir in the crème de cassis. Remove from the heat and set aside to cool completely.

2 Divide the Madeira cake evenly between 8 small glass dessert bowls. Spoon over about half the cooled berry mixture, making sure the juices soak into the cake.

3 Prepare the jelly in a jug according to the packet instructions, and divide it evenly between the trifle bowls.

4 In a mixing bowl, whisk the mascarpone until smooth, then beat in the vanilla extract. Gradually whisk in the custard until thick and velvety. Spoon the mascarpone custard evenly over each trifle. Top with the softly whipped cream. Chill for at least 2–3 hours, or overnight.

5 Just before serving, spoon the remaining berry mixture over, then finish with cherries on top.

Clodagh's Stress-Free Trifle Tips

1. Keep the mascarpone custard layer thick enough to sit clearly between the fruit and cream. If it feels loose, chill it briefly before layering.

2. The trifles are ideal to make the day before. Add the remaining berry mixture and cherries just before serving, so they look fresh and vibrant.

3. For a more indulgent version (it's Christmas, after all), drizzle an extra splash of crème de cassis or orange liqueur over the Madeira cake before adding the fruit.

BUTTERY ORANGE & BRANDY MINCE PIES

MAKES 18–24, DEPENDING ON SIZE

There's something quietly magical about a tray of homemade mince pies coming out of the oven in December. These are rich and crumbly, with a buttery, orange-scented pastry that brightens the sweetness while the brandied mincemeat adds warmth and depth, so each pie feels indulgent but perfectly balanced. They're ideal to bake ahead for the Christmas season, either kept in a tin for drop-in visitors or frozen and reheated so they taste as if they've just been made.

For the buttery orange pastry

250g (9oz) plain flour, plus more to dust
50g (1¾oz) icing sugar
180g (6oz) cold unsalted butter, chopped, plus more for the tin
Finely grated zest of 1 orange
1 egg yolk
2-3 tablespoons cold water
Fine sea salt

To fill and finish

2-3 tablespoons brandy, or to taste
About 400g (14oz) good-quality mincemeat
A little finely grated orange zest (optional)
1 egg, lightly beaten
Caster or icing sugar, to dust

1. Start by making the pastry: place the flour, icing sugar and a pinch of fine sea salt in a bowl and stir together. Rub in the cold butter with your fingertips (or pulse-blend in a food processor) until the mixture resembles fine crumbs. Add the orange zest, then mix in the egg yolk. Sprinkle over 2 tablespoons cold water and gently bring the dough together, adding the final tablespoon only if needed. Shape into a disc, wrap and chill in the refrigerator for at least 30 minutes.
2. Lightly butter a shallow bun or mince pie tin. Roll out the chilled pastry on a lightly floured work surface to about 3mm (1/8 inch) thick. Using a round cutter slightly larger than the holes in your tin, cut out bases and press them gently into the tin. Re-roll the trimmings and cut out smaller rounds, stars or other shapes for the tops.
3. In a bowl, stir the brandy into the mincemeat. If you'd like more citrus, add a little orange zest as well. Taste and adjust the level of brandy to your liking; the flavour will soften slightly once baked. Spoon a generous amount of the brandy-laced mincemeat into each pastry case, leaving a little space at the top as the filling will bubble in the oven. Place the pastry lids, stars or other shapes on top and press gently to secure. Brush lightly with beaten egg.
4. Chill the filled pies in the refrigerator for 15 minutes while you preheat the oven to 180°C fan (400°F), Gas Mark 6. Bake for 15-20 minutes, until the pastry is golden and the filling is gently bubbling. Leave in the tin for a few minutes, then transfer to a wire rack. Dust with caster or icing sugar just before serving.

INDEX

D

E

First published in Great Britain in 2026 by Kyle Books, an imprint of Octopus Publishing Group Ltd

Carmelite House
50 Victoria Embankment
London EC4Y 0DZ
www.octopusbooks.co.uk

An Hachette UK Company
www.hachette.co.uk

The authorized representative in the EEA is Hachette Ireland, 8 Castlecourt Centre, Dublin 15, D15 XTP3, Ireland (email: info@hbgi.ie)

Text copyright © Clodagh McKenna 2026
Photography copyright @ Issy Croker 2026
Additional photography on pages 9, 21, 26, 51, 135, 183, 209, 231 and 239 © Clodagh McKenna 2026
Design and layout copyright @ Octopus Publishing Group 2026

Distributed in the US by Hachette Book Group, 1290 Avenue of the Americas, 4th and 5th Floors, New York, NY 10104

Distributed in Canada by Canadian Manda Group, 664 Annette St., Toronto, Ontario, Canada M6S 2C8

All rights reserved. No part of this work may be reproduced or utilized in any form or by any means, electronic or mechanical, including photocopying, recording or by any information storage and retrieval system, without the prior written permission of the publisher.

Clodagh McKenna and Issy Croker have asserted their rights under the Copyright, Designs and Patents Act 1988 to be identified as the author and photographer of this work, respectively.

ISBN: 978 1 80419 454 6
eISBN: 978 1 80419 462 1

A CIP catalogue record for this book is available from the British Library.

Printed and bound in Europe.

10 9 8 7 6 5 4 3 2 1

Publisher: Joanna Copestick
Art Director: Yasia Williams
Project Editor: Lucy Bannell
Photographer: Issy Croker
Food and Prop Stylist: Emily Ezekiel
Lead Food Assistant: Sunita Parsons-Solomon
Food Assistant: Abigail Kaufman
Senior Production Manager: Katherine Hockley

ABOUT THE AUTHOR

Clodagh McKenna is a chef, TV presenter, best-selling cookbook author and entrepreneur who runs Broadspear, her 100-acre sustainable farm in the English countryside. She is the author of nine cookbooks, including the bestselling titles *In Minutes* and *Clodagh's Happy Cooking*, and is a much-loved resident chef on ITV's *This Morning*. Her new TV show, *Clodagh Cooking at Home*, airs later this year on ITV, bringing viewers even closer to her life, recipes and entertaining at Broadspear.

Over the past eight years at Broadspear, Clodagh and her husband Harry have transformed the land into a thriving, regenerative smallholding. They have restored a one-acre eighteenth-century walled vegetable and fruit garden, planted an orchard, established beehives and created wildflower meadows, cutting gardens and a pickling and fermenting shed (and a tiny pub). The farm is home to their hens, ducks, woodland pigs and Aberdeen Angus cattle, and it provides the inspiration and ingredients for Clodagh's seasonal recipes, entertaining ideas and homegrown lifestyle.

On screen, Clodagh has hosted five of her own television series, including *Fresh from the Farmers' Markets* and *Fresh from the Sea*, and she won ITV's *Cooking with the Stars* in 2022. Her warm, can-do approach has made her a trusted voice for anyone who wants to cook delicious food, celebrate the seasons and bring people together around the table, whether on busy weeknights or for big, joyful occasions.

As an entrepreneur, Clodagh is the founder of The Clodagh Store, her online lifestyle destination that brings the spirit of Broadspear into people's homes. Curated with the same care she applies to her cooking and hosting, the store features pieces for the kitchen and table, seasonal homeware and thoughtful gifts that reflect her love of craftsmanship, comfort and sustainable living. It is an extension of her ethos: to help people create homes that feel welcoming, lived in and ready to entertain at a moment's notice.

Clodagh has also built a large, engaged digital community who turn to her for everyday inspiration and escapism. Her upbeat recipe reels, glimpses of life on the farm and behind-the-scenes moments from her kitchen have earned her a dedicated following on Instagram, where she shares as @clodagh_mckenna. She continues the conversation on her YouTube channel too, with longer form videos that dive deeper into recipes, seasonal projects and life at Broadspear, inviting viewers to cook along, slow down and find joy in the simple rituals of home.

ACKNOWLEDGEMENTS

Harry Herbert, my darling husband. Thank you for your endless love, encouragement and for always believing in me and everything I do. You are at the heart of it all.

Jo Copestick, my wonderful publisher: this being our last book together makes it all the more meaningful. You have been such a guiding light across so many of my books, always listening, encouraging and bringing my ideas to life with such care and brilliance. I will treasure everything we've created together and will miss you more than words can say.

Emily Ezekiel, creative director of food styling and props. Your talent is truly extraordinary. Thank you for pouring your heart, creativity and magic into every detail of this book.

Issy Croker, photographer. My first book with you, and what a joy it has been. Thank you for your energy, and for capturing our home and recipes with such beauty and feeling.

Lucy Bannell, editor. Thank you for your dedication to this book and your incredible attention to detail, ensuring every recipe is so carefully double- and triple-checked.

Yasia Williams, designer: thank you for making every page feel so elegant, thoughtful and beautifully balanced.

Sunita Parsons-Solomon, lead home economist. Thank you for your incredible skill, warmth, your energy, and of course your wonderful playlists. You made every day in the kitchen such a joy.

Abigail Kaufman, assistant home economist, thank you for your support, care and hard work throughout. It has meant so much. You are pure joy!

Scarlet Furness, managing editor. Thank you for guiding everything so seamlessly and helping bring this book together so beautifully.

Lucy Brown and Erin Brown, PR and marketing: thank you for all your work behind the scenes and for helping share this book with such care and enthusiasm.

Katherine Hockley, production; thank you for your expertise and attention to detail in bringing the final book to life so beautifully.

The Broadspear team: Ana, Connor and Leo. Thank you for caring for the farm throughout the year. We are so grateful for your dedication, hard work and everything you do.

And to you, for buying this book, cooking the recipes and welcoming them into your home: thank you. Without your support, there would be no book.

Love,

Clodagh xx